THE ELEMENTS OF
WRITING ABOUT
LITERATURE AND FILM

Elizabeth McMahan
ILLINOIS STATE UNIVERSITY

Robert Funk
EASTERN ILLINOIS UNIVERSITY

Susan Day
ILLINOIS STATE UNIVERSITY

New York   San Francisco   Boston
London   Toronto   Sydney   Tokyo   Singapore   Madrid
Mexico City   Munich   Paris   Cape Town   Hong Kong   Montreal

Macmillan Publishing Company
866 Third Avenue, New York, New York 10022

Library of Congress Cataloging-in-Publication Data

McMahan, Elizabeth.
  The elements of writing about literature and film.

  Includes index.
    1. Literature—Research. 2. Moving-picture
criticism. 3. Criticism—Technique. 4. Exposition
(Rhetoric) I. Funk, Robert. II. Day, Susan.
III. Title.
PN81.M494 1988   808'.0668   87-21904
ISBN 0-02-327954-0

  02 03 04 DA   13 14 15

ISBN 0-02-327954-0

ACKNOWLEDGMENTS

"Do not go gentle into that good night," Dylan Thomas, *The Poems of Dylan Thomas*.
    Copyright 1952 by Dylan Thomas. Reprinted by permission of New Directions
    Publishing Corporation.
From "The Hollow Men," COLLECTED POEMS 1909–1962 by T. S. Eliot, copyright
    1936 by Harcourt Brace Jovanovitch, Inc.; copyright ©1963, 1964, by T. S. Eliot.
    Reprinted by permission of Harcourt Brace Jovanovitch, Inc. and Faber and Faber
    Limited.

ISBN 0-02-327954-0

Preface

This slim text contains the essentials for understanding and writing about literature and film. Despite its brevity, the book is comprehensive. Everything beginning students need to know in order to appreciate and write well about literature and film is here, clearly explained and abundantly illustrated.

The literary approach is mainly traditional (formalist), but reader response (subjective) critics will find that this book incorporates their insights as well. The chapter on film, which dovetails with the chapters on fiction, poetry, and drama, offers ample explanations of techniques that make the study of film unique. In the chapters devoted to writing instruction, film receives equal treatment with fiction, poetry, and drama.

The text is divided into two parts. The first section, "Analyzing Literature and Film," explains in four chapters how to go about understanding fiction, poetry, drama, and film. The second part, "Writing About Literature and Film," provides instruction in conventional literary writing and also encourages the use of writing during all phases of literary study—annotating texts, taking notes, jotting down reactions, drafting responses, writing to explore ideas. That is, it encourages writing as a mode of learning, as a means of sharpening critical thinking. Of course, it also includes traditional instruction on finding an approach, devising a thesis, organizing the ideas, and maintaining a critical focus, as well as offering advice about drafting, revising, quoting, documenting, proofreading, and editing.

By attending to the relationships among reading, writing, and thinking, this little book enables its users to integrate their developing appreciation of literature and film with their increasing abilities in thinking and writing—to the lasting benefit of both.

Our thanks to the many people who have helped us prepare this text: our perceptive reviewers—Nancy G. Anderson, Auburn University, Pauline Ann Buss, William Rainey Harper College, Carol Fairbanks, University of Wisconsin—Eau Claire, Catherine B. Kloss, University of Pittsburgh; our exemplary editor—Tony English; our efficient production chief, Barbara Chernow, and our colleagues and friends— Charles Harris, Michele Finley, Bill Weber, Dan LaSeure, David X Lee, and Mark Silverstein.

Elizabeth McMahan
Robert Funk
Susan Day

Contents

CONTENTS

PART ONE

Analyzing Literature and Film

The only reason for reading literature, observed Henry James, is that is does attempt to present life. By studying the artistic presentation of human experience in novels, short stories, poems, plays, and films, we try to find keys to understanding the meaning of our own experience. Or, to put it less grandly, we try to discover how better to muddle through the complex business of living. The resulting perceptions concerning human behavior make the serious study of literature worth the endeavor.

Examining literature and films provides both pleasure and knowledge. The knowledge stems from understanding the *theme* of the work, which usually provides some insight into the human condition. You will discover, though, that contemporary works often raise moral or ethical questions but make no pretense of providing answers. From these we learn more indirectly. Their value lies in pointing out important problems and inducing us to seek solutions.

You will find the study of literature and film more rewarding if you know the terminology used by critics as well as some of the useful approaches to critical analysis. You need to learn what questions to ask yourself as you examine a work—and how to determine the best answers to those questions. The first section of this book will provide the tools you need to achieve that understanding.

Chapter 1

Analyzing Fiction

In order to gain a complete understanding of a work of fiction (that is, a short story or a novel), you should read it twice. "Good grief," you say, "does that mean I have to read all the way through *War and Peace* a second time?" Perhaps not. But if you are studying a shorter work, you should try to find time to read it twice. And if you plan to write about a piece of fiction—even a novel as long as *War and Peace*—you must give it a second reading.

Preferably, let some time elapse between readings so that you can mull the piece over in your mind. Your initial reading can be purely for pleasure, but the second reading should involve study—careful and deliberate—of all the elements that combine to produce a unified whole. During that second reading you will want to underline key passages and make notes to yourself in the margins recording significant discoveries and personal responses.

Note the Structure

During the second reading, you should give some attention to the way the work is structured. The action, or *plot* (what happens), usually is spurred by some conflict involving the *protagonist* (the main character). Except in some modern works, most short stories and novels have a clear beginning, middle, and end, in which the conflict producing the action becomes increasingly intense, building to a climax that sometimes resolves the conflict, sometimes simply concludes it—often in catastrophe. Do not expect many happy endings in serious fiction. A somber conclusion is more likely.

Usually plots proceed in regular *chronological order*, following a time sequence similar to that in real life. But occasionally an author employs *flashbacks*, stopping the forward action to recount something which happened in the past, in order to supply necessary background material or to maintain suspense. Through a flashback in F. Scott Fitzgerald's *The Great Gatsby*, for instance, we learn of Jay Gatsby's humble beginnings—and of possibly sinister involvements in his rise to wealth. And if William Faulkner had written "A Rose for Emily" chronologically, without the distorted time sequence, he could never have achieved the stunning impact of his morbid conclusion.

Since structure means broadly the way a work is put together, try to discover a framework or pattern that shapes the piece into a unified whole. The structure of Nathaniel Hawthorne's *The Scarlet Letter* can be described as divided into three parts in which the action in each section relates to a crucial scene on the scaffold. But one critic sees the novel as structured in five parts, like a stage drama. Sometimes great works of fiction are more loosely put together. Hawthorne's *The Blithedale Romance*, for instance, is structured around the seasons, beginning with the promise of spring, which is ominously blighted by a blinding snowstorm, and ending in the fall, which conjoins the dying of nature with the suicide of Zenobia. The structure of Edith Wharton's *The House of Mirth* is even simpler: the novel chronologically follows episodes selected to reveal the plight of the lovely, ill-fated Lily Bart.

Subplots

Longer works, like novels, plays, and films, frequently include one or more *subplots*, which produce minor complications in the main action. Often some quality of a major character is illuminated through interaction with minor characters in a subplot. In a well-unified work, the action of a subplot serves to reinforce the theme. In Joseph Heller's scathing anti-war novel, *Catch 22*, the subplot involving Milo Minderbinder and his flourishing business empire satirizes the activities of corporate profiteers, who gained millions of dollars at the expense of the millions of people who died. Thus, the subplot strengthens Heller's powerful anti-war theme. Occasionally, though, subplots are introduced simply to provide interest, excitement, or comic relief. As you study a work involving subplots, consider how they function. Do they provide action that contributes to the overall success of the work? If so, try to decide how. You may find you can write an interesting paper by focusing on the way a subplot helps to develop character or theme.

Become Aware of Specialized Techniques

As you study a work on second reading, you may notice a number of important things that you missed the first time through. Sometimes you become so caught up in the action and so interested in the characters that you forget to pay close attention to the literary techniques. And some devices, like irony and foreshadowing, by their very nature, are difficult to perceive on first reading.

Irony

Situational irony involves an upsetting of expectations—having the opposite happen from what we would anticipate. Sometimes we can recognize irony at once. In Stephen Crane's novel, we can see that Henry Fleming's "red badge of courage" is ironic as soon as he receives the wound, because he is running from battle at the time. But only after reflecting on the novel do we become aware of the pervasiveness of the irony. Once we notice the repeated pattern of Henry's romantic delusions being undercut by hard realities, we can deduce that the ending also is ironic—that Henry has learned little from his experiences and remains a dreamer. Often we simply need to know the outcome of an action in order to detect the irony. In Flannery O'Connor's story "Good Country People," for example, the fact that the intelligent, sophisticated, well-educated Hulga-Joy is duped by the bumpkin bible salesman is intensely ironic, but we do not realize that this will happen until the end of the story.

Verbal irony is discussed under tone on pages 13–14. Dramatic irony is discussed in our chapter on drama, page 47, but can occur in any work of imaginative literature.

Foreshadowing

Another literary device that becomes much more apparent on second reading is *foreshadowing*. We may not know the signficance of various hints and suggestions until the events they foreshadow finally occur. The unusual spring snowstorm at the beginning of Hawthorne's *The Blithedale Romance* foreshadows Zenobia's death at the end in two ways: cold kills the promise of the spring buds (as death ends the promise of her vibrant life); and her corpse is described as cold and white (like the cold whiteness of the snowstorm). Eventually we discover that even the title of the novel is ironic, since the concluding events are far from being blithe (happy), and all hope of romance is gone. When we go through a second reading, both irony and foreshadowing become far more apparent and can contribute significantly to our understanding and appreciation of the work.

Images, Motifs, Symbols

Be alert also for *images*—for words and phrases that appeal to the senses and often put a picture in your mind. We can classify images roughly into several categories:

visual—images of sight ("she looked bloated, like a body long submerged in motionless water"—William Faulkner)

auditory—images of sound ("the pounding of the cylinders increased: ta-pocketa-pocketa-pocketa-*pocketa-pocketa*"—James Thurber)

olfactory—images of smell ("the frailest of ringlets, still black, with an odor like copper"—Eudora Welty)

kinetic—images of motion ("her dress swung as she moved her body and the soft rope of her hair tossed from side to side"—James Joyce)

thermal—images of hot or cold ("stony hills ablaze with heat"—Stephen Crane)

tactile—images of texture and touch ("the bristly hairs rubbed painfully against her breast"—Yukio Mishima)

Such images increase the enjoyment of reading fiction and, if deliberately repeated, can become *motifs* that emphasize some important idea in the story. The constant images of fungus and decay in Edgar Allan Poe's "The Fall of the House of Usher" reinforce our impression of the deterioration of Roderick Usher's mind.

If a repeated image gathers significant meaning, it then becomes a *symbol*—to be clearly related to something else in the story. The moldering of the Usher mansion probably symbolizes the decay of Usher's psyche, just as the repeated images of dust and decay in Faulkner's "A Rose for Emily" symbolize the deterioration of Miss Emily's mind as well as the fortunes of her once prosperous family.

Archetypal Symbols. Some symbols are considered *archetypal*, or universal, conveying the same meaning in all cultures from the time of earliest civilization. For example, the circle is an ancient symbol of wholeness or perfection; the sea has for centuries symbolized the voyage through life; a bird is an archetypal symbol for the soul; water suggests cleansing; white is associated with purity; spring means rebirth. "How am I supposed to know all of these things?" you may well ask. Luckily, there exists a handy volume that allows you to look up words to discover their symbolic significance:

J. E. Cirlot's A *Dictionary of Symbols* (New York: Philosophical Library). Your library will have a copy in the reference section.

Phallic and Yonic Symbols. Two important and commonly employed symbols are associated with human sexuality. A *phallic* symbol suggests the potency of the male or the force of male dominance in a patriarchal society. Common phallic symbols are guns, spurs, snakes, columns, towers, sleek cars, jet planes—objects resembling in shape the male sex organ. A *yonic* symbol suggests the fecundity of the female or the allure of female sexuality. Common yonic symbols are caves, pots, glasses, cups, rooms, full-blown roses, pompom chrysanthemums—round or concave objects resembling the shapes of the primary sex organs of the female. If you think of fruit, bananas are phallic, apples are yonic.

Remember, though, that these objects will not always be charged with sexual significance. You must be sure that the image can be reasonably associated with sexuality. In Kate Chopin's *The Awakening*, the "full, fragrant roses" adorning Edna's table at the climactic birthday dinner party can be seen as emphasizing the culmination of her sexual maturity. And in the final scene, the phallic image of the waves, "coiled like serpents about her ankles," unites with the auditory images—her father's voice and the cavalry officer's clanging spurs—to suggest the patriarchal forces of society which ultimately defeat her.

For discussions of *metaphor, paradox,* and *sentimentality,* see Chapter 2.

Consider Point of View

Sometimes the *point of view*—the manner in which an author chooses to tell what happens—can be crucial to the effectiveness, sometimes even to the understanding, of a work of fiction. Since several different systems exist for classifying and describing point of view in fiction, we will explain here the most commonly used terms.

Omniscient Author

Often the point of view in a fictional work will be straightforward. An *omniscient* (all-knowing) *author* chooses which details to include, which character's thoughts to reveal, and presents the narrative as if telling a story to the readers. Most eighteenth- and nineteenth-century novels, until the time of Henry James, were written from an omniscient point of view. Occasionally these authors, including James, will address their readers directly as "dear reader" or "gentle reader," in order to gain a sense of immediacy. Here is an example of omniscient point of view from Katherine Anne Porter's short novel, *Noon Wine.*

> . . . the boys referred to their father as the Old Man, or the Old Geezer, but not to his face. They lived through by main strength all the grimy, secret, oblique phases of growing up and got past the crisis safely if anyone does. Their parents could see they were good solid boys with hearts of gold in spite of their rough ways. Mr. Thompson was relieved to find that, without knowing how he had done it, he had succeeded in raising a set of boys who were not trifling whittlers. They were such good boys Mr. Thompson began to believe they were born that way, and that he had never spoken a harsh word to them in their lives, much less thrashed them. Herbert and Arthur never disputed his word.

Limited or Jamesean

Henry James is credited with devising a variation on the omniscient author approach wherein the point of view is conveyed primarily through the consciousness of a single character, usually the main character. The readers are given the thoughts of this central character in detail but know nothing of the thoughts of the other characters. In *Daisy Miller,* for example, we are privy to endless debates in Winterbourne's mind concerning Daisy's respectability—or lack of it. But we are never told what Daisy thinks, because to

know her thoughts would be to know the solution to Winterbourne's dilemma.

Unreliable Narrator. The limited point of view often includes the added challenge of dealing with an *unreliable
narrator*, since the central character, through whose consciousness the story or novel is filtered, is often self-deceived.
In James's short novel *The Beast in the Jungle*, John Marcher
thinks of himself as a caring, sensitive person. He seems
charming, and readers can easily be deceived into seeing him
as he sees himself. But in describing Marcher's relationship
with May Bartram, the woman who loves him, James supplies
several hints that Marcher is totally self-centered and uncaring
about anyone besides himself:

> It was one of his proofs to himself, the present he made her on
> her birthday, that he hadn't sunk into real selfishness. It was
> mostly nothing more than a small trinket, but it was always fine
> of its kind, and he was regularly careful to pay more for it than
> he thought he could afford.

Even as May is dying, Marcher continues to try to take from
her instead of giving her the love she needs:

> It sprang up sharp to him, and almost to his lips, the fear she
> might die without giving him light. He checked himself in time
> from so expressing his question.

At the end of the novel Marcher finally gains self-knowledge
and admits to himself that "he had never thought of
her . . . but in the chill of his egotism and the light of her
use." Reading this work a second time, we can see that James
has carefully prepared us for "John Marcher's arid end," but
on first reading we may well be taken in by the skillfully
presented, biased viewpoint of the central character.

First Person

Some authors choose to let one character tell the story
from a *first person* point of view, as Huck does in *Adventures
of Huckleberry Finn*. Part of our pleasure in reading this

novel derives from our engagement with Huck, who seems so real, so earnest, so in need of our sympathy as he relates his adventures in his own voice as if speaking directly to the reader. And the effectiveness of the meaning of the novel derives largely from the boy's innocent, nonjudgmental narration. He describes the behavior of the adults he encounters on his journey but never draws any moral. We are allowed to observe the greed, the lust, the prejudice, the hypocrisy, the general moral miasma—and judge for ourselves.

A slightly different version of the first person child-narrator occurs in James Joyce's "Araby." This story recounts the experience of a young boy whose illusions are shattered by a tawdry reality, but the whole thing is told from the perspective of the boy as a grown man. This point of view allows the author to speculate with an adult's wisdom (using an adult's vocabulary) on the childhood experience.

Of course, first-person narrators are usually adults describing their own adult experiences or adventures. Here is a brief passage from Charlotte Perkins Gilman's "The Yellow Wall-Paper," in which the first-person narrator, a woman descending into madness, records her thoughts in a journal:

> If a physician of high standing, and one's own husband, assures friends and relatives that there is really nothing the matter with one but temporary nervous depression—a slight hysterical tendency—what is one to do?
>
> My brother is also a physician, and also of high standing, and he says the same thing.
>
> So I take phosphates or phosphites—whichever it is—and tonics, and journeys, and air, and exercise, and am absolutely forbidden to "work" until I am well again.
>
> Personally, I disagree with their ideas.
>
> Personally, I believe that congenial work, with excitement and change would do me good.
>
> But what is one to do?

Sometimes the first-person narrator is not the protagonist but an observer reporting the action, a peripheral character who is present during all the events but is not the one to whom things are happening. In Somerset Maugham's story "Rain," the doctor makes a perfect first-person peripheral narrator. As a physician he has been trained in accurate observation, and as a character not directly involved in the conflict, he provides a convincingly unbiased report of the action.

Dramatic or Objective

The *dramatic* or *objective* point of view, most often found in short stories, narrates action but does not report or comment on anyone's thoughts or feelings. Ernest Hemingway, in "Hills Like White Elephants," uses this type of narration, allowing his characters to tell the story themselves through conversation, almost as if on stage.

> "Oh, cut it out."
> "You started it," the girl said. "I was being amused. I was having a fine time."
> "Well, let's try and have a fine time."
> "All right. I was trying. I said the mountains looked like white elephants. Wasn't that bright?"
> "That was bright."
> "I wanted to try this new drink. That's all we do, isn't it—look at things and try new drinks?"
> "I guess so."
> The girl looked across at the hills.
> "They're lovely hills," she said. "They don't really look like white elephants. I just meant the coloring of their skin through the trees."
> "Should we have another drink?"
> "All right."

This point of view has the advantage of keeping authorial comment entirely out of the work, leaving readers to evaluate the fiction entirely on their own.

Stream of Consciousness

Stream of consciousness narration attempts to represent the thoughts running through a character's mind without the ordering imposed by the conscious mind. In Katherine Anne Porter's "The Jilting of Granny Weatherall," the stream of consciousness point of view (in this case, Granny's) perfectly conveys the distorted impressions and nostalgic recollections drifting in and out of the dying woman's mind. In this passage her daughter Cornelia is caring for her as she remembers another daughter, Hapsy, who died years before.

> It was Hapsy she really wanted. She had to go a long way back through a great many rooms to find Hapsy standing with a baby on her arm. She seemed to herself to be Hapsy also, and the baby on Hapsy's arm was Hapsy and himself and herself, all at once, and there was no surprise in the meeting. Then Hapsy melted from within and turned flimsy as gray gauze and the baby was a gauzy shadow, and Hapsy came up close and said, "I thought you'd never come," and looked at her very searchingly and said, "You haven't changed a bit!" They leaned forward to kiss, when Cornelia began whispering from a long way off, "Oh, is there anything you want to tell me? Is there anything I can do for you?"

Observe the Setting

The setting of a piece of fiction, like the point of view, can sometimes be of consequence, sometimes not. *Setting* includes the place and time during which the action occurs. In Willa Cather's *My Ántonia*, the bleak Nebraska landscape so influences the lives of the characters that the novel simply could not be set in a less harsh environment. Likewise, the nineteenth-century time period is essential because Cather is recounting the experiences of pioneers. The brooding heaths of Thomas Hardy's Wessex novels are equally central to those works, as the grim landscape seems almost to precipitate the tragic consequences that befall the characters. And again, the nineteenth-century setting is crucial, since the novels deal with social and moral issues which have changed appreciably since that time. Both the dark forest setting and the communal atmosphere of the village carry symbolic significance in Nathaniel Hawthorne's "Young Goodman Brown."

As you study a work of fiction, give some thought to the setting. Could the events just as well take place somewhere else? Or does the setting seem to play an integral part? Would the work be changed significantly if set in a different time? Does either setting or time period contribute importantly to the meaning of the story?

Discover the Mood and Tone

Setting often exerts a powerful influence on the mood (or atmosphere) of a work. *Mood* refers to the emotional effect aroused in the readers by the setting and the events. Mood is that chill foreboding that Poe creates by setting "The Fall of the House of Usher" in a remote, moldering mansion on the edge of a black, stagnant pool and then having eerie things happen. Shirley Jackson uses mood ironically to increase the impact of "The Lottery" by conveying the atmosphere of a summer picnic just before turning her story abruptly toward ritual murder.

The word *tone*, sometimes used interchangeably with mood and atmosphere, can more usefully denote the attitude of the writer toward the subject or material being written about. If a writer is having fun with a subject, the tone might be described as wry, playful, light, or humorous—one of the easiest tones to identify. If a writer is serious about a subject, the tone might be called somber, solemn, or perhaps serious—also an easy tone to identify. If, on the other hand, you find the tone of a work quite difficult to detect, it probably is not important in analyzing the work and can simply be called neutral. A neutral tone, by the way, is quite common in fiction.

Verbal Irony

The tone you must be most careful not to overlook involves *verbal irony*. An ironic tone is created through subtle verbal clues. Since words used ironically suggest the opposite of their literal meaning, to miss the ironic tone is to mistake the meaning. Consider the tone of this passage from Kate Chopin's *The Awakening*:

> The mother-women seemed to prevail that summer at Grand Isle. It was easy to know them, fluttering about with extended, protecting wings when any harm, real or imaginary, threatened their precious brood. They were women who idolized their children, worshipped their husbands, and esteemed it a holy privilege to efface themselves as individuals and grow wings as ministering angels.

Since motherhood is a quality usually much admired in our society, we realize—if we catch the irony—that Chopin is suggesting that motherhood can be overdone. The verbal clues are the words conveying the image of mother as brooder hen: the *extended, fluttering wings* (which metamorphose comically into angel wings) protecting the *precious brood*. Also, the exaggeration of the words elevating motherhood to a religion—*idolized, worshipped, holy privilege*—suggests that Chopin questions the appropriateness of such dedication. The most obvious clue to the irony is, of course, the mention of protection from both real and *imaginary* harm.

Think About Style

All of the elements discussed so far affect the style of a work, especially tone, imagery, and point of view. But, specifically, style refers to an author's choice of words and how those words are arranged to present the material. Sometimes rhythm is important. Do the words come in short, stacatto bursts, in the manner of Ernest Hemingway?

> Ten cars were lined up side by side under the long shed. They were top-heavy, blunt-nosed ambulances, painted gray and built like moving vans. The mechanics were working on one out in the yard. Three others were up in the mountains at dressing stations.
>
> —*A Farewell to Arms* (1929)

Or do they flow in a liquid smoothness, in the manner of Virginia Woolf?

> A steamer far out at sea had drawn in the air a great scroll of smoke which stayed there curving and circling decoratively, as

if the air were a fine gauze which held things and kept them
softly in its mesh, only swaying them this way and that.

—*To the Lighthouse* (1927)

In order to analyze style, you need to consider sentence
length and complexity. Does the writer use primarily short,
fairly simple sentences, like Hemingway in the previous example, or long, circuitous, involved sentences, like Henry James?
Here is a sentence typical of James's style in his later years:

> It was characteristic of the inner detachment he had hitherto so
> successfully cultivated and to which our whole account of him
> is a reference, it was characteristic that his complications, such
> as they were, had never yet seemed so as at this crisis to thicken
> about him, even to the point of making him ask himself if he
> were, by any chance, of a truth, within sight or sound, within
> touch or reach, within the immediate jurisdiction, of the thing
> that waited.

—*The Beast in the Jungle* (1903)

Of course, this use of unusual sentence patterns and an ele-
vated diction makes his style easy to identify. Because they
employ neither, Mark Twain and Sherwood Anderson are
described as writing in the "plain style," a label considered
complimentary by those who admire an easy, graceful, and
unpretentious way with words. Here is a passage from a short
story by Sherwood Anderson:

> Neither of us had ever seen a woman's body before. It may have
> been the snow, clinging to the frozen flesh, that made it look
> so white and lovely, so like marble. No woman had come with
> the party from town; but one of the men, he was the town
> blacksmith, took off his coat and spread it over her. Then he
> gathered her into his arms and started off to town, all the others
> following silently. At that time no one knew who she was.

—"Death in the Woods" (1926)

You will scarcely ever need to look up a word when reading
Twain or Anderson, but when reading Edgar Allan Poe, you
need a dictionary handy because of his fondness for latinate
words.

Poe's interest in creating mood certainly accounts in large

measure for his choice of words, images, and descriptive details. Notice in the following passage how skillfully he amasses details to create a bleak, depressing atmosphere of "irredeemable gloom," as the narrator first encounters the cadaverous Roderick Usher:

> The room in which I found myself was very large and lofty. The windows were long, narrrow, and pointed, and at so vast a distance from the black oaken floor as to be altogether inaccessible from within. Feeble gleams of encrimsoned light made their way through the trellised panes, and served to render sufficiently distinct the more prominent objects around; the eye, however, struggled in vain to reach the remoter angles of the chamber, or the recesses of the vaulted and fretted ceiling. Dark draperies hung upon the walls. . . . I felt that I breathed an atmosphere of sorrow. An air of stern, deep, and irredeemable gloom hung over and pervaded all.

The details are singularly foreboding: the dark draperies, black floors, and inaccessible windows admitting only feeble light; the vaulted ceiling providing a suggestion of entombment; and perhaps the finest touch, the "gleams of encrimsoned light" casting an infernal glow over the scene.

Consider also the importance of dialect in conveying verisimilitude, a feeling of reality, in a work of fiction. In "A Summer Tragedy," Arna Bontemps presents an aged black couple, a sharecropper and his wife, both in ill health and hopelessly in debt, who have made a suicide pact rather than suffer the indignity of going to the poorhouse. The authenticity of their dialect makes the story believable and thus heightens the pathos:

> "How many bale o' cotton you think we got standin'?" she said.
> Jeff wrinkled his forehead as he calculated.
> "'Bout twenty-five, I reckon."
> "How many you make las' year?"
> "Twenty-eight," he said. "How come you ask that?"
> "I's jes thinkin'," Jennie said quietly.
> "It don't make a speck o' difference though," Jeff reflected. "If we get much or if we get little, we still gonna be in debt to old

man Stevenson when he gets through counting up agin us. It's
took us a long time to learn that."

If you have read *Huckleberry Finn*, you will remember that
a great deal of the humor stems from Huck's uneducated
dialect in the narrative voice:

> After supper she got out her book and learned me about Moses
> and the Bulrushers; and I was in a sweat to find out all about
> him; but by-and by she let it out that Moses had been dead a
> considerable long time; so then I didn't care no more about him;
> because I don't take no stock in dead people.

Analyzing style involves looking at words—at their arrangement into sentences as well as their meanings and connotations. You need to do a close and careful examination of
virtually every component of a work in order to thoroughly
describe the style.

Study the Characters

As you reread the work, pay special attention to the dialogue,
those passages in quotation marks that characters speak to
each other. You can begin to determine characterization from
these exchanges, just as you come to know real people partly
by what they say. As you form an understanding of a character, you also need to notice what other people in the story
say about that person, how they respond to that person, as
well as what the author reveals of that person's thoughts and
past behavior. Since fiction often allows us access to what
the characters are thinking and feeling, we can sometimes
know fictional persons better than we do our closest friends
and family members.

Motivation

As you analyze characters, consider their *motivation*, their
reasons for doing the things they do. Sometimes we can be
certain of a character's motivation for behaving in a certain
way; at other times this motivation becomes one of the ele-

ments we must figure out before we can fully appreciate the story. Our judgment of Sammy, the narrator of John Updike's "A & P," depends upon an analysis of his motives for quitting his job. Does he do it just to impress the three girls who come into the store? Is he really protesting the shabby way the manager treats the girls (as Sammy says he is)? Or is he taking advantage of an opportunity to leave a job he hates? Perhaps his motives are mixed. In any case, our evaluation of Sammy's motivation is central to our understanding of Sammy—and to our interpretation of the story.

Foils

Minor characters, called *foils*, often function as contrasts for main characters, thus heightening our understanding of the major characters. In *Huckleberry Finn*, Tom Sawyer, with his boyish foolishness and heedless trickery, serves to point up the growing maturity and basic honesty of Huck Finn. Sometimes foils play roles that also help to illuminate theme. In Jack London's "To Build a Fire," the dog, who instinctively knows better than to cross the Arctic when the temperature is fifty below, serves as a foil for the foolish, egocentric man. At the same time, the dog, as a creature of nature, emphasizes London's theme of the insignificance of human beings in the face of implacable natural forces.

Static and Dynamic Characters

The terms *static* and *dynamic* are used as labels to denote characters who do not change throughout the course of a work (static) and those whose experiences alter them (dynamic). Henry Fleming in *The Red Badge of Courage* is a good example of a static character, because he is just as visionary and deluded at the end as he was at the beginning. Edna Pontieller in *The Awakening* is a good example of a dynamic character because she is a totally different person after she experiences her dual awakening to sexuality and selfhood.

Significance of Names

Some authors give their characters names that carry significance. If you look up "Ahab" and "Ishmael" in a dictionary
of biblical characters, you will find that Melville's Ahab and
Ishmael share meaningful traits with their biblical counter-
parts. The name of Henry James's heroine Daisy Miller suits
her perfectly: "daisy" suggests her natural, unspoiled innocence and charm; "miller" suggests her common, far from
aristocratic origins. In the same work, Winterbourne's name
suggests his frigid manner, for he ultimately frosts poor Daisy.
Names will not always have meaning, of course, but you
should consider the possibility.

Continue Questioning to Discover Theme

Your entire study of these various elements of fiction—all
the questions you ask of yourself and then seek to answer—all
of this critical thinking should lead to an understanding of
the meaning, the *theme*, of the story. The title may in some
way point toward or be related to the meaning. If you ask
yourself why Katherine Mansfield entitled her poignant story
"Bliss," you will probably decide that she was being ironic—
that she wanted us to see how fleeting is the young wife's
blindly trusting happiness. Sometimes the title identifies the
controlling symbol, as in John Steinbeck's "The Chrysanthemums" and Charlotte Perkins Gilman's "The Yellow Wall-
paper." Joseph Conrad's title *The Heart of Darkness* directs
us straight to his theme: the evil that lurks at the core of
human experience.

You need to ponder everything about a work of fiction in
order to discover its theme. Keep asking yourself questions
until you come up with some meaningful observation about
human behavior or the conduct of society. The questions
that follow will guide you in exploring any novel or short
story and perhaps spark that essential insight which leads to
understanding.

LIST OF QUESTIONS FOR ANALYZING FICTION

The following questions should help you understand any short story, novella (short novel), or novel. Some will have more bearing than others, depending upon the individual work. If you are preparing to write about a piece of fiction, you can generate most of the material for your paper by writing out your answers.

1. Who is the main character (the protagonist)? Does this person's character change during the course of the work? Do you feel sympathetic (favorable) toward the main character? If not, how do you respond? What sort of person is he or she?

2. Why are the minor characters there? Do any of them serve as foils? Consider each one individually.

3. Are the names of the characters significant?

4. Can you see a pattern in the way the plot is constructed? That is, can you describe the way the events are organized? Does the author use flashbacks? If so, for what purpose? Does surprise play an important role in the plot? Is there any foreshadowing?

5. Is anything about the work ironic? Consider verbal ironies as well as ironic situations.

6. How does imagery function? Are there repeated images (motifs)?

7. Do any of these images gather symbolic meaning? Is there, perhaps, a controlling symbol (like the river in *Huckleberry Finn*)?

8. What is the setting—the time period and the location? How important are these elements in the work? Could it be set in another time and place just as well?

9. Is the mood (or atmosphere) important? If so, try to describe it. How does the author create this mood?

10. Consider point of view: Who is the narrator? Is the narrator reliable? What effect does the point of view have on your response to the work? What would be gained or lost if the point of view were different—told by another character, for instance, or told in the first person?

11. Does the author's style affect your response to or your understanding of the work? If so, how would you describe the style? For example, what is the tone? Is it ironic, satirical, somber, light, wry, humorous, or simply neutral? Is the sentence construction fairly simple or elaborate? Can you detect a rhythm? Are the words familiar or fancy? Does the style create a mood? Do you think the style is important in contributing to the effectiveness of the work?

12. How does the title relate to the work? Does it give you a clue about the meaning?

13. What is the theme? Can you state it in a single sentence? How is this meaning conveyed? In other words, how did you figure it out?

Chapter 2

Analyzing Poetry

The language of poetry is far more compressed than the language of fiction. The pleasure of reading poetry derives from the beauty of the language—the delight of the sounds and the images, as well as the power of the emotion and the depth of the insights conveyed. Although poetry may seem difficult at first, it can also be intensely rewarding.

In order to enjoy discovering the meaning of poetry, try to approach it with a positive attitude—with a willingness to understand. Poetry invites your creative participation. More than any other form of literature, poetry allows you as reader to inform its meaning as you bring your own knowledge and experience to bear in interpreting images, motifs, symbols, and metaphor.

Read the Poem Out Loud

Begin by reading the poem aloud. Rhyme and rhythm work in subtle ways to emphasize key words and clarify meaning. As you reread, go slowly. Pay careful attention to every word; examine any difficult parts several times.

Get the Literal Meaning First

Before you begin interpreting a poem, you need to be sure that you understand the literal or surface meaning.

Straighten Out the Syntax

Since one of the delights of poetry stems from the unusual ways in which poets put words together, you may sometimes need to straighten out the syntax. For instance, Thomas Hardy writes,

> And why unblooms the best hope ever sown?

The usual way of expressing that question would be something like this:

> And why does the best hope ever sown not bloom?

You should rewrite in what is called a *paraphrase* every unclear line so that the whole poem makes sense.

Fill in Any Blanks

Occasionally you may need to fill in words that the poet has deliberately omitted through *ellipsis*. When Walt Whitman writes,

> But I with mournful tread,
> Walk the deck my Captain lies,
> Fallen cold and dead,

we can tell that he means "the deck [*on which*] my Captain lies,/ Fallen cold and dead."

Sometimes, though, an ellipsis can be much more challenging than that one—as well as crucial to understanding the meaning. Consider this stanza by Emily Dickinson:

> He put the Belt around my life—
> I heard the Buckle snap—
> And turned away, imperial,
> My Lifetime folding up—
> Deliberate, as a Duke would do
> A Kingdom's Title Deed—
> Henceforth, a Dedicated sort—
> A Member of the Cloud.

Clearly the most demanding line in that verse is the last one. What in the world does "A Member of the Cloud" mean? Before you even begin to answer that question, you should first be sure that you have the syntax straight for the whole stanza.

Write a Prose Version

The best way to make sure of the literal meaning is to write out a version for your own use that fills in all of the ellipses and puts the sentences into our normal word order (subject/verb/complement). With Emily Dickinson, you also need to insert standard punctuation. Your clarified version might come out something like this:

> He put the belt around my life;
> I heard the buckle snap.

Both lines are perfectly clear on the literal level. But now you have to decide which one "turned away." Since "he" is obviously the one in control, "he" would be the more logical choice for behavior described as "imperial." So, you would continue,

> And he turned majestically away,
> Folding up my lifetime
> Deliberately, as a duke would fold up
> The title deed of a kingdom.

Now, the most challenging part: from the last two lines the poet has omitted both subject and verb. So, you must decide whether the ellipsis should be filled in this way:

> Henceforth, I will be a dedicated sort of person,
> A member of the cloud,

or this way:

> Henceforth, he will be a dedicated sort of person,
> A member of the cloud.

You make the decision according to which version best fits the meaning of the preceding lines. Since the speaker (the

"I" in the poem) seems to be a woman describing the way her life has been restricted by a man (the imperial "he" who "put the belt around my life"), you will probably decide in favor of the first version. She is likely to be the one who will need to show dedication to him, since he clearly has power over her. Then, once you are sure of the literal meaning of the stanza, you can begin to speculate about what that unusual last line—"A Member of the Cloud"—could mean.

Pay Attention to Punctuation

Ordinarily you should pay close attention to the punctuation and capitalization in a poem. Both can provide clues to meaning. When Dylan Thomas writes,

> And you, my father, there on the sad height,
> Curse, bless, me now with your fierce tears, I pray,

we can tell that he means his real, not his heavenly father, because he did not capitalize "father."

But be advised that some poets, like Emily Dickinson and Stevie Smith, employ punctuation in eccentric ways or, like e e cummings and Nikki Giovanni, employ little or no punctuation at all. Along with the deliberate fracturing of syntax, this departure from standard punctuation comes under the heading of *poetic license* (freedom granted to literary artists to depart from the usual rules governing punctuation and usage).

Use Your Dictionary

You must always look up any words that you do not know—as well as any familiar words that fail to make complete sense in the context. When you read this line from Whitman,

> Passing the apple-tree blows of white and pink in the orchards,

the word "blows" seems out of place. If you consult your dictionary, you will discover a rare definition of blows: "masses of blossoms," a meaning that fits exactly.

Make Associations for Meaning

Once you understand the literal meaning of a poem, you can begin to expand that meaning into an interpretation. As you do so, consider the following questions: Who is the speaker? Who is being addressed? What is the message? What do the images add? What do the symbols suggest? How does it all fit together? What is the theme?

When, for instance, Emily Dickinson in the following lines envisions "Rowing in Eden," how do you respond to this image of a rowboat in the Garden?

> Rowing in Eden—
> Ah, the Sea!
> Might I but moor—Tonight—
> In Thee!

Can she mean literally rowing in Eden? Not unless you picture a lake in the Garden, which is, of course, a possibility. What do you associate with Eden? Complete bliss? Surely. Innocence, perhaps—the innocence of Adam and Eve before the Fall? Or their awakened sensuality after the Fall? Given the opening lines of the poem,

> Wild Nights—Wild Nights!
> Were I with thee
> Wild Nights should be
> Our luxury!

one fitting response might be that "Rowing in Eden" suggests gliding through sexual innocence in a far from chaste anticipation of reaching the port of ecstasy: to "moor—Tonight—/In Thee!"

Study the Devices of Poetry

Many aspects of fiction and drama occur also in poetry. While paradoxes appear in fiction and even in the nonfiction prose of some writers, you will encounter them more frequently in poetry. And while the connotations of words are important in fiction, you must become especially sensitive to their emotional messages when reading poetry. Knowing who is speaking (the persona) and noticing the attitude of the speaker (the tone) are just as important in poetry as in prose. In order to identify these elements, you need to ask yourself questions about the poem.

Identify the Persona

A good question to begin with is this: Who is the speaker in the poem? Often the most obvious answer seems to be "the poet," especially if the poem is written in the first person. When Emily Dickinson begins,

> This is my letter to the world
> That never wrote to me—

we can be fairly sure that she is writing in her own voice—that the poem itself is her "letter to the world." But poets often adopt a *persona*; that is, they speak through the voice of a character they have created. Stevie Smith, herself a middle-aged woman, adopts a persona of a different age and of the opposite sex in these lines:

> An old man of seventy-three
> I lay with my young bride in my arms. . . .

Readers of "Song of Myself" recognize that even though the poet speaks in the first person and names himself,

> Walt Whitman, a kosmos, of Manhattan the son,
> Turbulent, fleshy, sensual, eating, drinking and breeding

he presents himself as an expansive, complex persona who represents all people everywhere, a cosmos indeed. The speaker in W. H. Auden's "The Unknown Citizen" is apparently a spokesperson for the bureaucracy—but most certainly is not Auden himself. Thus, in order to be strictly accurate, you should avoid writing, "The poet says . . ." and use "The speaker in the poem states . . ." or "The persona in the poem says . . ."

Discover the Tone

After deciding who the speaker is, your next question might be, "What is the tone of this poetic voice?" *Tone* in poetry is essentially the same as in fiction: the attitude of the writer toward the subject matter of the poem. Tone in a piece of writing is similar to the tone of voice in speaking. If a friend finds you on the verge of tears and comments, "You certainly look cheerful today," the tone of voice—as well as the absurdity of the statement—lets you know that your friend is being ironic—that she means the opposite of what she says. In the same way, when Stephen Crane begins a poem,

> Do not weep, maiden, for war is kind,

any alert reader perceives the ironic tone at once from the word "kind," which war definitely is not. But irony can, of course, be much more subtle. Sometimes you need to put together a number of verbal clues to be sure of the irony.

One of your challenges in identifying tone involves finding exactly the right word or words to describe it. Even after you have detected that a work is ironic, you sometimes need to decide whether the irony is gentle or bitter, whether the work is light or scathing in tone. You need a number of adjectives at your command in order to be precise. As you analyze tone, these terms may prove useful in describing it: humorous, joyous, playful, light, hopeful, brisk, lyrical, admiring, celebratory, laudatory, expectant, wistful, sad, mournful, maudlin, dreary, lugubrious, tragic, elegaic, solemn, somber, poignant, earnest, blasé, disillusioned, straightforward, curt, hostile, sarcastic, sardonic, cynical, ambivalent.

Consider the Connotations

Many words have *connotations*—emotional associations— that can strongly affect their literal meanings. Although "female parent" and "mother" have the same denotative meaning, the terms are not interchangeable because of their connotations, the emotions—or lack of emotion, in the case of "female parent"—aroused in the reader. Emily Dickinson writes wistfully of "a last communion in the haze." Consider how different that line would be if she had written, "a last communion in the smog."

Interpret the Paradoxes

A statement that at first appears contradictory but turns out to be true is called a *paradox*. The motto of Mary, Queen of Scots, for instance, was "In my end is my beginning"—a clear contradiction if taken literally. But, considered in the light of Christian doctrine, the motto becomes an assertion of faith in an afterlife and hence true for the believer. Simon and Garfunkel sing of "the sounds of silence," and we, the listeners, are left to figure out how silence can have sound. Most paradoxes in poetry are like this last example: they require thoughtful, imaginative interpretation before we can discover their truth.

Oxymorons.   An extreme paradox expressed by juxtaposing contradictory terms is called an *oxymoron*. When Walt Whitman speaks of "the sweet hell within," he refers to the joy and agony combining within his being to produce poetry.

Learn to Interpret Figurative Language

To a far greater extent than either fiction or drama, poetry relies upon various types of figurative language to enrich its meaning. You need to learn about these figures of speech in order to become a sensitive reader of poetry.

Metaphor and Simile

Perhaps the most characteristic feature of poetry is the use of metaphorical language. A *metaphor* is an imaginative comparison in which two unlike things are compared by means of one element they have in common. When Shakespeare writes, "Thy eternal summer shall not fade," he compares the youth and beauty of his lover to the joys of summer. Technically, an imaginative comparison introduced by *like* or *as* or *than* can be called a *simile*: "My love is like a red, red rose," says Robert Burns. Of course, metaphor can emphasize the grim as well as the lovely. Wilfred Owen, writing about the agonies suffered by soldiers in World War I, speaks of "blood-shod" feet. Randall Jarrell, describing the death camps of World War II, tells of corpses "stacked like sodden wood."

Sometimes metaphors can be sophisticated and elusive. You need to make associations, just as you do with imagery, in order to grasp the meaning. When Dylan Thomas says, "The force that through the green fuse drives the flower,/ Drives my green age," you can see that the image of the "green fuse" represents the stem of a flower. But what does "my green age" mean? Ask yourself what "green" brings to mind. Grass is green, foliage is green, but that association is not much help. If you look up the word "green" in your dictionary, you will discover that it can also mean "youthful" and "brand-new." Ah, and now you remember that being "green" at something means being new and inexperienced, a greenhorn. So, "my green age" means "my youth" or "my early years." The theme of that same poem is stated more simply by Bob Dylan when he sings, "Everything not busy being born is busy dying."

Images, Motifs, and Symbols

Although we discussed imagery, motifs, and symbolism in the chapter on fiction, these devices lie at the very heart of poetry interpretation. Imagery contributes substantially to the delight of poetry and engages our imagination as we seek to discover meaning. Often poems are constructed around a controlling image, like that of the spider and its web in Whitman's "A Noiseless Patient Spider" or the cherry tree in A. E. Housman's "Loveliest of Trees." Especially in longer poems, images are repeated in patterns or motifs. And, just

as they do in fiction, images that accumulate meaning function as symbols—like Whitman's spider or William Butler
Yeats's holy city of Byzantium. You might want to review
our discussion of imagery and symbolism in the previous
chapter; we cannot stress too strongly their importance in
achieving a sensitive response to poetry.

Synesthesia. One quite specialized figure of speech occurs more often in poetry than in fiction—*synesthesia*, which
describes one sensory image in terms of other senses. Emily
Dickinson uses synesthesia in describing a fly as moving
against a window pane with "blue uncertain stumbling buzz."
The word "blue" begins a visual image, the "uncertain stumbling" adds motion, and the "buzz" gives it sound.

Personification

Those of us who love animals are so accustomed to
personification—giving human characteristics to nonhuman
things—that we scarcely notice the figure of speech when
Robert Frost says of the little horse,

> He gives his harness bells a shake
> To ask if there is some mistake.

We take more notice of personification, though, when poets
give human traits to nonliving things, as Anne Sexton does
when she says, "Daylight is nobody's friend," or as T.S. Eliot
does in saying, "the afternoon, the evening, sleeps so peace-
fully." We can also see that personification involves a
metaphor—in these examples daylight is compared to a friend
and the late afternoon to a person quietly sleeping.

Allusions

Sometimes poems, like novels, stories, and plays, contain
allusions (indirect references to famous persons, events,
places, or to other works of literature) that add to the meaning.
The significance of characters' names, mentioned in the previous chapter, forms one kind of allusion. In poetry, allusions

can be fairly easy to perceive. When Eliot's J. Alfred Prufrock, in his famous love song, observes,

> No! I am not Prince Hamlet, nor was meant to be,

we know that he modestly declines to compare himself with Shakespeare's Hamlet, a character who also had difficulty taking decisive action. Many allusions, though, are more subtle. And, to begin with, you must be familiar with the work being alluded to in order to catch an allusion. You must know these lines from Ernest Dowson,

> Last night, ah, yesternight, betwixt her lips and mine,
> There fell thy shadow, Cynara!

or you will, of course, miss the allusion to them in Eliot's "The Hollow Men":

> Between the motion
> And the act
> Falls the shadow.

And you will miss the reinforcement of meaning conveyed by the allusion—the poignant sense of loss and desolation conveyed by Dowson's lines.

But do not think that all allusions are obscure; many of them can be looked up in standard reference books. If, for instance, you are puzzled by Algernon Swinburne's line,

> Thou hast conquered, O pale Galilean,

your trusty dictionary will identify the Galilean as Jesus Christ. For less well-known figures or events, you may need to consult a dictionary of biblical characters, a dictionary of classical mythology, or a good encyclopedia.

Useful Reference Works

Other valuable reference tools are Sir James Frazer's *The Golden Bough*, which discusses preclassical myth, magic, and religion; and Cirlot's A *Dictionary of Symbols*, which traces through mythology and world literature the significance of various archetypal (universal) symbols—the sea, the seasons, colors, numbers, islands, serpents, and a host of others. At the end of this text you are reading, you will find a more extensive list of useful reference books.

Notice Sentimentality

Having warm, sentimental feelings about your friends and loved ones is fine, but sentimentality means something quite different—and negative—when applied to literature. In literary criticism, *sentimentality* means that the writer is trying desperately to drag an emotional response from the readers by playing on stock responses—appeals to emotionally charged conditions or situations that usually arouse deep feelings, such as motherhood, childhood, patriotism, peace, marriage, childbirth, and the death of a child. These are, of course, also the stuff about which great literature is written. The difference lies in the exaggeration of the appeal. The emotion of the writer is no doubt sincere in sentimental verse, but heartfelt emotion produces far more bad poems than good ones. You can see that in the following stanza, Eliza Cook wants us to weep with her over "The Old Arm-Chair," but we are much more likely to laugh at her excesses:

> I love it, I love it! and who shall dare
> To chide me for loving that old arm-chair?
> I've treasured it long as a sainted prize,
> I've bedewed it with tears, I've embalmed it with sighs,
> 'Tis bound by a thousand bands to my heart;
> Not a tie will break, not a link will start.
> Would you know the spell?—a mother sat there!
> And a sacred thing is that old arm-chair.

Greeting cards can also be brazenly sentimental. You need to become sensitive to these unrestrained emotional appeals and recognize them as examples of bad writing.

Consider the Forms of Poetry

All poetry has *form*—that is, it has design or structure. While many elements go into making the forms of poetry, they all involve arranging the words in patterns. Sometimes sound controls the pattern; sometimes the number of words or the length of lines determines the form.

Rhythm and Rhyme

Sound effects are produced by organized repetition. Systematically stressing or accenting words and syllables produces *rhythm*; repeating similar sounds in an effective scheme produces *rhyme*. Both effects intensify the meaning of a poem, arouse interest, and give pleasure. Once we notice a pattern of sound, we expect it to continue, and this expectation makes us more attentive to the subtleties in the entire poem.

Rhythm can affect us powerfully. We respond almost automatically to the beat of a drum, the thumping of our heart, the pulsing of an engine. Poetic rhythm, usually more subtle, is made by repeating stresses and pauses. (See Figure 2-1 for a description of the most common poetic rhythms.) Rhythm conveys no verbal meaning itself but, when used skillfully, it reinforces the meaning and tone of a poem. Consider how Theodore Roethke captures the raucous spirit of "My Papa's Waltz" in the recurring three-stress, waltzing rhythm of these lines:

> ˘ ´ ˘ ´ ˘ ´
> We romped until the pans
> ´ ˘ ˘ ´ ˘ ´
> Slid from the kitchen shelf
> ˘ ´ ˘ ´ ˘ ´
> My Mother's countenance
> ˘ ´ ˘ ´ ˘ ´
> Could not unfrown itself.

Rhyme, a recurring pattern of similar sounds, also enhances tone and meaning. Because rhymed language is unusual language, it helps to set poetry apart from ordinary expression and calls attention to the sense, feeling, and tone of the words. Rhyme also gives pleasure by fulfilling the expectation of the sound patterns. Usually dependent on sound, not spelling, rhyme occurs when accented syllables contain the

same or similar vowel sound with identical-sounding consonants following the vowel: *right* and *bite, knuckle* and *buckle.*
Rhymes are commonly used at regular intervals within a
poem, often at the ends of lines:

> Yet he wasn't a scab or odd in his views,
> For his Union reports that he paid his dues.

Alliteration, Assonance, and Consonance

Closely allied to rhyme are other verbal devices that depend
upon the correspondence of sounds. *Alliteration* is the repetition of consonant sounds at the beginning of words or in
stressed syllables:

> Should the *glee—glaze—*
> In Death's—*stiff—stare—*

Assonance is the repetition of similar vowel sounds that are
not followed by identical consonant sounds: *grave* and *gain,
shine* and *bright. Consonance* is a kind of half-rhyme in
which the consonants are parallel but the vowels change:
blade and *blood, flash* and *flesh.* Alliteration, assonance, and
consonance can occur frequently but usually not in regular,
recurring patterns like rhyme. These devices do, though, like
rhyme, please the ear, accent the meaning, and affect the
tone, melody, and tempo of poetic expression.

Stanzaic Form: Closed and Open Forms

In the past, almost all poems were written in *closed form*:
poetry with lines of equal length arranged in fixed patterns
of stress and rhyme. Although these elements of form are
still much in evidence today, modern poets prefer the greater
freedom of *open form* poetry, which uses lines of varying
length and avoids fixed patterns of rhyme and rhythm.

Rhyme Schemes and Stanzas. Closed forms, although
challenging for the poet to control, give definition and shape
to poetic expression. Rhyme schemes and stanza patterns

Figure 2-1 PROSODY

RHYTHM. Read the poem aloud to determine basic patterns of stressed and unstressed sounds.

⏑ = Unstressed

╱ = Stressed

A stressed sound and its nearby unstressed sounds are called a FOOT. The feet are labeled according to the prevailing pattern of stressed (╱) and unstressed (⏑).

NAME	FOOT	EXAMPLE
IAMBIC (iamb)	⏑ ╱ a a	⏑ ╱ ⏑╱ ⏑ ╱⏑ ╱ The Chief Defect of Henry King ⏑ ╱⏑ ╱⏑ ╱ ⏑ ╱ Was chewing little bits of string. (Hillaire Belloc)
TROCHAIC (trochee)	╱ ⏑ a a	╱ ⏑╱⏑╱ ⏑ ╱ ⏑╱ ⏑ Once upon a time I spent a summer (Henry Taylor)
DACTYLIC (dactyl)	╱ ⏑ ⏑ a a a	╱ ⏑ ⏑ ╱ ⏑ ⏑ ╱ ⏑ That is no country for old men. (W.B. Yeats)
ANAPESTIC (anapest)	⏑ ⏑ ╱ a a a	⏑ ⏑ ╱ ⏑ ⏑ ╱ ⏑ ⏑ ╱ ⏑ It was sad, oh so fondly to love him (Alexander Kerr)
SPONDAIC (spondee)	╱ ╱ a a	╱ ╱ ╱ ╱ Stop that! heartbreak

LINE LENGTH. Count the number of feet in each line.

monometer—one foot

dimeter—two feet

trimeter—three feet

tetrameter—four feet

pentameter—five feet

hexameter—six feet

Figure 2-1 PROSODY *(continued)*

Combine the prevailing rhythm and line length to name the
METER.

Iambic pentameter:

˘ ´ ˘ ´ ˘ ´ ˘ ´ ˘ ´
When my love swears that she is made of truth
˘ ´ ˘ ´ ˘ ´ ˘ ´ ˘ ´
I do believe her, though I know she lies.
(Shakespeare)

Dactylic tetrameter:

´˘ ˘ ´˘ ˘ ´ ˘ ´
Only my Daddy could look like that,
˘ ´ ˘ ˘ ´˘ ˘ ´ ˘ ˘ ´˘
And I love my Daddy like he loves his Dollar.
(William Jay Smith)

---

demand the careful arrangement of words and lines into units
of meaning that can guide the reader in understanding the
poem. Stanzas can be created on the basis of the number of
lines, the length of the lines, the pattern of stressed syllables
(the meter), and the rhyme scheme (the order in which
rhymed words recur).

Since the metrical patterns (called *scansion*) used to mark
rhythm in English verse were devised not for English but for
Greek verse, the system seldom works too well (a lot like
traditional English grammar, which was devised to describe
not English but Latin). Thus, we prefer a loose approach to
scansion—marking the stressed and unstressed syllables but
not dividing the lines into feet.

The simplest stanza form is the *couplet*: two rhymed lines,
usually of equal length and similar meter. Oliver Wendell
Holmes's "The Chambered Nautilus" is written in rhyming
couplets, although the lines vary in length and in rhythm:

Build thee more stately mansions, O my soul,

As the swift seasons roll! . . .

Let each new temple, nobler than the last,

Shut thee from heaven with a dome more vast,

Till thou at length art free,

Leaving thine outgrown shell by life's unresting sea!

The most common stanza in English poetry is the *quatrain*, a group of four lines with various rhyme schemes. To identify a rhyme scheme, you call the first rhyme *a*, the second one *b*, the third one *c*, and so on. Whenever a rhyme recurs, you give it the same letter it was assigned initially, like this:

Western wind, when wilt thou blow,	(*a*)
The small rain down can rain?	(*b*)
Christ, if my love were in my arms	(*c*)
And I in my bed again!	(*b*)

—Medieval lyric, anonymous

Here is a quatrain employing rhyming couplets:

When the stars threw down their spears,	(*a*)
And watered heaven with their tears,	(*a*)
Did he smile his work to see?	(*b*)
Did he who made the lamb make thee?	(*b*)

—from "The Tyger," William Blake

And this quatrain has an alternating pattern:

The whiskey on your breath	(*a*)
Could make a small boy dizzy;	(*b*)
But I hung on like death:	(*a*)
Such waltzing was not easy.	(*b*)

—from "My Papa's Waltz," Theodore Roethke

Longer stanza patterns are used, of course, but the quatrain and the couplet remain the basic components of closed form poetry.

Sonnets. The fixed form that has been used most frequently by famous poets in England and America is the
sonnet. Originating in Italy in the fourteenth century, the
sonnet became a staple of English poetry in the sixteenth
century and has continued to attract practitioners ever since.
The basic form of the *sonnet* is firmly fixed: fourteen lines,
with ten syllables per line, arranged in a set rhyme scheme.
The *Italian sonnet*, not found often in English poetry, has
eight lines in the first stanza (the octave) and six in the second
(the sestet). The popular *Shakespearean sonnet* has three
quatrains followed by a couplet and rhymes *a b a b, c d c d,
e f e f, g g*. The early sonnets were often love poems, but
contemporary poets use the form quite effectively with mark-
edly different content.

Free Verse. A poem written in open form generally has
no rhyme scheme and no basic meter that can be followed
through the entire selection. Rhyme and rhythm do occur,
but not necessarily in regular patterns. Many readers think
that open form poetry is easy to write, but that is not the
case. Only careless poetry is easy to write, and even closed
forms can be badly done. Open forms demand their own
special arrangements; without the fixed patterns of traditional poems to guide them, modern poets must discover these
structures on their own. Eliot's "The Love Song of J. Alfred
Prufrock" demonstrates how open form still uses sound and
rhythm to reinforce tone, enhance meaning, and guide the
responses of the reader. Notice in the following lines how
Eliot employs a humorous rhyme to convey tone (*flicker/
snicker*), and how the brief, final line emphasizes Prufrock's
extreme timidity:

> I have seen the moment of my greatness flicker,
> And I have seen the eternal Footman hold my coat, and
>   snicker,
> And in short, I was afraid.

Syntax

Poets often manipulate for various effects the form of their sentences. For instance, the short, staccato sentences of Gwendolyn Brooks's "We Real Cool" ("We real cool. We/ Left school. We/ Lurk late. We/ Strike straight. We/Sing sin. We/Thin Gin. We/Jazz June. We/Die soon.") impress us in a way entirely different from the effect of the intricate expression of Robert Frost's sonnet "The Silken Tent," in which a single sentence stretches over fourteen lines (see page 99). Some poets deliberately fracture the syntax of the normal English sentence to achieve unusual effects. e e cummings, for example, forces his readers to pay close attention to the line "anyone lived in a pretty how town" by rearranging the words in an unexpected way. In the standard pattern for an exclamation, the line would read, "How pretty a town Anyone lived in!"

Speculate on Theme

Robert Frost remarked that "Poetry begins in delight and ends in wisdom." After experiencing the delight of a poem, you often need to study it carefully in order to derive its wisdom, which we call theme.

You discover theme in poetry essentially the same way you do in fiction: by reading the work carefully and repeatedly while asking yourself pertinent questions. The responses to these questions should lead you eventually to the meaning of the poem.

LIST OF QUESTIONS FOR ANALYZING POETRY

1. Can you paraphrase the poem?
2. Who is the speaker in the poem? How would you describe this persona?

3. What is the speaker's tone? Which words reveal this tone? Is the poem perhaps ironic?

4. What heavily connotative words are used? What words have unusual or special meanings? Are any words or phrases repeated? If so, why? Which words do you need to look up?

5. What images does the poet use? How do the images relate to one another? Do these images form a unified pattern (a motif) throughout the poem?

6. What figures of speech are used? How do they contribute to the tone and meaning of the poem?

7. Are there any symbols? What do they mean? Are they universal symbols, or do they arise from the particular context of this poem?

8. What is the theme (the central idea) of this poem? Can you state it in a single sentence?

9. How important is the role of sound effects, such as rhyme and rhythm? How do they affect tone and meaning?

10. How important is the contribution of form, such as rhyme scheme and line arrangement? How does the form influence the overall effect of the poem?

Chapter 3

Analyzing Drama

A play is written to be performed. Although most drama begins with a written script, the author of a play counts on the collaboration of others—actors, directors, set designers, costumers, makeup artists, lighting and sound engineers—to help translate the written words into a performance on stage. (The same is true in producing film or videotape, as we will explain in the next chapter.) Unlike novelists and poets, playwrights do not necessarily expect their words to be read silently. They expect their words to be spoken by actors and heard by an audience. They also hope that the director and the actors will give an inspiring visual interpretation of their words.

Listen to the Lines

The major difference between reading and watching a play is that, as reader, you do not have the actors' voices and gestures to interpret the lines and establish the characters for you. Because playwrights rely largely on speeches or conversations (called *dialogue*) to define character, develop plot, and convey theme, it will be your task as a reader to listen to the lines in your mind. Read the dialogue to yourself as you would expect to hear it spoken. For example, when you read Antigone's response to Creon,

> Your edict, King, was strong,
> But all your strength is weakness itself against
> The immortal unrecorded laws of God,

you should hear the assurance and defiance in her voice. Or when you read Tom's farewell speech to his sister in *The Glass Menagerie*, you should detect the mixture of tenderness and regret in his words:

> Oh, Laura, Laura, I tried to leave you behind me but I am more faithful than I intended to be! . . . Blow out your candles, Laura—and so goodbye. . . .

Of course the tone of these lines is not as clear when they are taken out of context, but even these brief quotations illustrate the charged nature of language you should expect when you read a play.

You can actually read the lines out loud to yourself or enlist some fellow students to act out some scenes with you. These oral readings will force you to decide how to interpret the words. But most of the time you will have to use your imagination to re-create the sound of the actors' voices.

Reading a play does have significant advantages over viewing a live performance. Unlike a theatergoer, a reader can stop and return to lines or speeches that seem especially complicated or meaningful. Close reading gives you the opportunity to examine and consider the playwright's exact words, which often fly by quickly, sometimes i.1 altered form, in an actual performance.

Visualize the Scene

In addition to imagining the dialogue, you will also want to picture what is supposed to be happening on stage. Movement, gesture, and setting are all important in the performance of a play. These nonverbal elements of the language of drama are conveyed in the author's *stage directions*, the italicized parts set off in brackets or parentheses. Especially in medieval and Renaissance plays, you will also find the cues for gestures, movements, and facial expressions in the character's words themselves. For example, these lines of Othello, spoken when he has been roused from his bed by a fight among his men, suggest the physical performance that would accompany the words:

> For Christian shame, put by this barbarous brawl:
> He that stirs next to carve for his own rage
> Holds his soul light; he dies upon his motion.
> Silence that dreadful bell.

Reading this speech with an actor's or director's imagination, you can see in your mind the character stride angrily into the fight scene, gesture threateningly at the men who are poised to continue the fight, and then point suddenly offstage in the direction of the clamoring alarm bell. Such a detailed reading will take time, but you will be rewarded by the satisfaction of catching the full dramatic quality of the play.

In more recent times, playwrights like Arthur Miller and Tennessee Williams have tried to keep artistic control over the interpretation of their works by including detailed stage directions in their scripts. The extensive production notes for Williams's *The Glass Menagerie* sometimes read like descriptions from a novel or a poem:

> Friday evening. It is about five o'clock of a late spring evening which comes "scattering poems in the sky." A delicate lemony light is in the Wingfield apartment. . . . A fragile, unearthly prettiness has come out in Laura: she is like a piece of translucent glass touched by light, given a momentary radiance, not actual, not lasting.

With or without notes like this, your imagination will be working full time when you read a play. You will be rewarded by the freedom to produce the play in the theater of your own mind.

The Staging of Drama

In your study of fiction and poetry, you have already practiced most of the skills necessary to analyze drama. A second reading continues to be important in this genre also in order to detect irony and foreshadowing. Understanding a few terms and techniques that are unique to drama will also increase your abilities to study and enjoy this kind of literature.

Types of Stages

The traditional theater in which the audience sits out front while the actors perform on a raised stage separated from the viewers by a curtain (and perhaps an orchestra) is called a *proscenium stage*. Technically, the arch from which the curtain hangs is the proscenium; the space extending from the bottom of the curtain to the footlights is called the apron. The stage directions in italics in plays that you read indicate where the playwright wants the actors to move. Upstage means toward the back; downstage means toward the apron. A traditional set (made of canvas-covered frames called flats) will look like a room—with one wall removed for the audience to see through. Sometimes, though, the set will be constructed to resemble the battlements of a castle, an opening in a forest, or a lifeboat on the ocean. Occasionally the setting is only suggested: a character climbs a ladder to deliver lines supposedly from a balcony or from an upstairs room. In one modern play, the two protagonists are presented on a bare stage speaking throughout the production (with only their heads visible) from inside garbage cans.

Another kind of stage, called *theater in the round* or an *arena stage*, puts the audience in raised seats on all sides with the players performing in the round space in the middle. After the audience is seated, the lights are extinguished, and the actors enter through the same aisles used earlier by the audience. When the actors are in position, the lights come up, illuminating only the stage, and the play begins. At the end of a scene or an act, the lights go down again, signifying the fall of the curtain and allowing the actors to leave. Stagehands come on between acts or scenes, if needed, to rearrange the setting. Not all plays are suited to this intimate staging, of course, but the audience at an arena production gains an immediacy, a feeling almost of being involved in the action, that cannot be achieved in a proscenium theater.

Production Techniques

Both stage and screen directors sometimes make exciting and daring alterations when producing a work. By changing the locale, the era, and the costumes, a director can bring an entirely different flavor to an old, familiar play. At Illinois State University's Shakespeare Festival, director Cal Pritner delighted audiences by doing *Twelfth Night* with 1930s costumes and art deco sets. Instead of Shakespearean lyrics, the fool sang Hoagy Carmichael songs and (with a cigarette clinging to his lower lip) accompanied himself on the piano. In the film *Throne of Blood*, director Akira Kurosawa presented Shakespeare's Macbeth as a nineteenth-century samurai warrior, with admirable results. If you have a chance to see an unconventional production of a play or a film, the contrast with the traditional interpretation could provide a focus for your writing.

Props

Sometimes the *props* (the properties, or articles used by the players) can be symbolic and thus will influence your interpretation of the drama. In Henrik Ibsen's *Hedda Gabler*, for instance, General Gabler's pistols, which figure prominently in the action, are clearly phallic symbols and can be seen to represent the strong masculine influence that shaped Hedda's life and defined her expectations. Ask yourself, then, why the play is called *Hedda Gabler*—although her married name is really Hedda Tesman—and you further realize the importance of her upbringing and the significance of the General's pistols.

Dramatic Irony

Identifying irony is just as important in drama as in fiction, poetry, or film. You should know about a special kind of irony characteristic of stage productions. *Dramatic irony* occurs when one or more characters are unaware of information that is known to other characters and to the audience or the readers. In Susan Glaspell's *Trifles*, the plot focuses on finding the murderer of a lonely woman's husband. The sheriff and his men, who are in the home searching for clues, pass over her sewing box repeatedly because they consider such women's "trifles" beneath their attention. The audience and the female characters are keenly aware that the very evidence the men seek lies hidden in that sewing box, placed there by the wife. The fact that the audience knows more than the investigators do creates the irony. The effectiveness of the play stems largely from this pervasive dramatic irony and the resulting tension and suspense, as the audience waits to discover what brand of justice will be served.

The Structure of Drama

You have already learned of the many forms that poetry can take. Dramatic structure is far less various, having followed almost the same pattern from the beginning. More than 2,000 years ago the Greek philosopher Aristotle pointed out that the most important element of drama is the *plot*, which should have a beginning, a middle, and an end. As obvious as this observation seems, it emphasizes the dramatist's need to engage an audience early, to keep it engaged throughout, and to satisfy its need for closure in the conclusion.

Recognizing the drama's strict time limits, Aristotle set down a number of conditions for developing a plot. The heart of the dramatic story, he declared, is the *argument*, and the conflict surrounding this argument creates tension and incites interest. The two sides of the conflict are represented on stage by the *protagonist*—the hero—and the *an-*

tagonist—the villain. The protagonist may be one person or many, and the antagonist may be a person, a group, or even a force (supernatural or natural). In Arthur Miller's *Death of a Salesman*, for instance, the antagonist may be the materialistic society in which Willy Loman struggles to survive.

Components of the Plot

The fundamental struggle between the protagonist and the antagonist is developed according to a set pattern that theater audiences have come to recognize and expect. This conventional structure can be varied, of course, and often is in modern plays, but most dramas contain the following elements:

1. *Exposition*—the revelation of facts, circumstances, and past events. Establishing the essential facts about the characters and the conflict can be accomplished in a number of ways. Often plays begin with characters revealing information through conversation. Sometimes a playwright simply begins at the story's beginning and allows the audience to discover what is going on at the same time the characters do. Or the action can begin in the middle of things (*in medias res*), perhaps even near the end, and gradually reveal the events that have already taken place. (In *Macbeth*, for instance, we learn of the protagonist's battlefield triumphs and honors.)

2. *Rising action*—the building of interest through complication of the conflict. (Macbeth encounters the witches; their prophecies are partially fulfilled; Duncan comes to Macbeth's castle; Lady Macbeth learns of the prophecies and spurs her husband on; Macbeth stabs Duncan; the king's sons flee and Macbeth is proclaimed king.)

3. *Climax*—the turning point of the play; can be a single moment or a series of events, but once reached, it becomes a point of no return. (Macbeth arranges to have Banquo and his son killed; the scheme succeeds only partially—Fleance escapes.)

4. *Falling action*—the unraveling of the plot during which events fall into place and the conflict moves toward final resolution. (Macbeth becomes distraught and seeks out the witches; Malcolm gathers forces to challenge Macbeth; Macbeth has Macduff's family murdered; Macduff joins Malcolm; Lady Macbeth goes mad.)

5. *Denouement*—the conclusion; the explanation or outcome of

the action; literally, "the untying." (Macduff confronts Macbeth and kills him; the riddles of the prophecies become clear; Malcolm is hailed as the new king.)

The denouement marks the end of the play: the lovers kiss, the bodies are carried offstage, and the audience goes home. Even when dramatists mix in other devices, rearrange elements, and invent new ways to present their material, they still establish a conflict, develop both sides of the argument, and reach a credible conclusion. After centuries of theater history, hundreds of plays still follow this pattern.

The Evolution of Dramatic Protagonists

Drama, like short stories and novels, provides us with carefully drawn examples of human speech and behavior. We come to an understanding of the characters in a play in much the same way that we analyze the characters in fiction. We pay attention to what they say and do—as well as to what others say about them and how others react to them. We examine their motivation and we look for foils, just as we do in analyzing fiction. But in analyzing drama, we add another dimension to the discussion of character. Besides referring to main characters and minor characters, we may speak of tragic heroes. Like the structure of drama, this concept has been with us since the fourth century B.C.

The Tragic Hero

Aristotle described the classic concept of the *tragic hero* as one "who is highly renowned and prosperous," a noble person who is inevitably destroyed because of a *tragic flaw*. This character flaw usually involves an excess of pride, greed, jealousy, envy, indecision, or lust. The Aristotelian definition implies that there is a natural, right ordering and proportion of characteristics within a human being which, if out of balance, causes calamity. Oedipus falls because his overwhelming pride (hubris) prevents him from seeing clues that are perfectly apparent to other characters and to the audience. Antigone, some critics argue, meets her tragic fate because of her extreme willfulness in defending her beliefs.

The Modern Hero

Aristotle's concept of the tragic hero served fairly well to define the role of protagonists until the twentieth century, when dramatists began writing plays about common, everyday people. In 1949 playwright Arthur Miller challenged the idea that the hero must be "a highly renowned and prosperous" figure who exhibits a tragic flaw. No longer can catastrophe be blamed exclusively on human character flaws, according to Miller. Instead, the idea of the modern hero involves a clash between the character and the environment, especially the social environment. Miller holds that each person has a chosen image of selfhood and social position; tragedy results when the character's environment denies the fulfillment of this self-concept. Thus, the hero no longer must be born into the nobility but gains stature in the action of pitting self against society. Feelings of displacement or indignity, then, are the driving forces for the modern tragic hero. In Miller's play *Death of a Salesman*, the main character, Willy Loman, imagines himself as a well-liked, successful, worldly business-man. Tragically, he is actually an object of ridicule and contempt, always on the edge of poverty. Such conflicts be-tween ideal self-image and reality form the central conflict of many modern plays.

Recent Developments in Drama

Taking Miller's idea of human disillusionment a step further, numerous dramatists in the latter half of the twentieth century have produced plays in which human existence is portrayed as basically absurd. These playwrights have created startling differences from the traditional representation of events as we view them on stage in plays such as *The Glass Menagerie* and *Death of a Salesman*.

Theater of the Absurd

The absurdist playwrights attempt to show that the human condition is itself absurd, pointless—especially when the social order is based on empty rituals that serve as insulation against life's unpleasant realities. Eugene Ionesco in *The Bald Soprano* emphasizes the banality of comfortable middle-class people by presenting characters who do nothing throughout the play except talk earnestly about the obvious—declaring as an observation of great insight, for instance, that life in the city is less peaceful than in the country. Samuel Beckett often departs from a realistic setting to exaggerate the absurdity of life, which must end in death. His play *Endgame* is the one in which two main characters inhabit garbage cans on an otherwise empty stage. Harold Pinter employs more realistic settings, but his plots involve the characters in menacing situations beyond their comprehension, and their incongruous behavior often lacks any conventional motivation. The mindset shared by absurdist playwrights is that the human predicament is anguished, meaningless, and futile.

Theater of Cruelty

In the 1930s the French director and playwright Antonin Artaud conceived a ceremonial kind of drama that subordinates words to action, gesture, and sound in an effort to overwhelm the spectators and liberate their instinctual preoccupations with crime, cruelty, and eroticism. Artaud's search for a theatrical means of generating existential awareness inspired many avant-garde directors and playwrights, such as Peter Weiss, who incorporated sounds, mime, and "happenings" into his play *Marat/Sade*.

Immediate Theater

Artaud's advice to "throw away the script" also led to a mode of dramatic presentation that features much improvisation and participation from the audience. Called *Immediate Theater* (or *Living Theater*), this style of performance achieved serious development in the 1960s under Polish playwright/director Jerzy Grotowski and British directors Joan Littlewood and Peter Brook.

LIST OF QUESTIONS FOR ANALYZING DRAMA

1. What is the central conflict in the play? How is it resolved?

2. Does the play contain any secondary conflicts (subplots)? How do they relate to the main conflict?

3. Does the play follow a traditional dramatic structure? Where does the climax occur? Is there a denouement?

4. Who is the main character or protagonist? What sort of person is he or she? Does this protagonist have a fatal flaw? Is the protagonist a hero?

5. Is the antagonist—the one who opposes the main character—a person, a social force, or an environment? If the antagonist is a person, does he or she cause conflict intentionally?

6. Do the other characters provide exposition (background information)? Are they used as foils to oppose, contrast, criticize, and thus help develop the main characters?

7. What are the time and setting of the play? How important are these elements? Could the play be set just as effectively in another time or place?

8. Is there foreshadowing? Is there irony? Is there any dramatic irony?

9. Are any of the elements in the play symbolic? Does the title provide any clue to understanding the play? Are the names of any of the characters significant?

10. What is the theme of the play? Can you state it in a single sentence?

11. Is the play a tragedy, a comedy, or a mixture? Is this classification important?

12. Is the presentation a realistic one? Does the playwright use any special theatrical devices? If so, what effect do they have on your impression of the play?

Chapter 4

Analyzing Film

Your background in literary analysis, enhanced by studying our first three chapters, will be of great help when you want to analyze a film. In fact, a popular introductory film textbook is entitled *How to Read a Film*. Although watching a film, of course, has obvious differences from reading, you will discover that often literary terms and approaches can be applied to the study of film. We will also discuss new terms and techniques that you need to know in order to understand film and write well about it.

The Structure of Film

Many, many films follow the traditional dramatic structure you studied in Chapter 3: exposition, complication, climax, falling action, denouement. Screenplays made from traditional novels, stories, and stage plays are especially likely to fit this plan. The film *Who's Afraid of Virginia Woolf?* (1966) is a good example. The stage version takes place in one setting, while the film version (thanks to the camera's freedom of movement) changes settings. The dramatic structure, however, remains the same in both versions. Original screenplays like *The Dirty Dozen* (1967) or *E.T.—The Extraterrestrial* (1982) also follow familiar dramatic structures.

Camera Work

In film, structure can be determined through camera work. Exposition—the part that supplies the basic information we need to understand what is going on—is often done with an establishing shot, a wide view (long shot) in which place, time, and often characters are revealed, in something like a painting. The camera then shifts to a closer view as the action begins. The establishing shot in a cowboy movie often pans and tracks (moves across and along) the main and only street of a western town; then the camera takes us to the sheriff's office, the saloon, the whorehouse, or wherever the first scene takes place.

Editing

Transitions between structural elements, which are marked by scene changes, curtains, and blackouts on stage, are marked by editing techniques in film. One scene can slowly disappear as the next materializes (a dissolve); a scene can fade to a blank or an almost blank screen before the next image appears (a fade); one scene can peel or twirl away, revealing the next underneath (a wipe); one image can simply end and the next begin (a cut). A number of other transitional techniques, obvious and subtle, mark structural shifts.

Flashbacks

In both literature and film we take notice when the expected structure is *not* followed. Some works of literature, like Porter's "The Jilting of Granny Weatherall" and Miller's *Death of a Salesman*, deliberately disrupt the chronological order of events in flashbacks to earlier events. When we analyze the work, part of our job is to explain why. In *Salesman*, for example, the time sequence is interrupted to show how the main character, Willy Loman, retreats into fantasies of the past as his present diminished life closes in on him.

Similarly, the film *Citizen Kane* employs flashbacks to contrast the simplicity and warmth of the main character's childhood with the emotional desolation of his adult success. *A Soldier's Story* (1983) consists of flashbacks as an investigator probes the murder of a black sergeant in the South. Each man interviewed provides a segment of the crime's history, and these segments are powerfully presented in flashbacks.

Crosscutting

Some literary works have a structure that alternates in presenting two plots, two settings, or two main characters. *The Grapes of Wrath* alternates narrative chapters about the Joad family with expository chapters about the power of nature over human beings and the power of capitalist greed over nature. Film lends itself extremely well to such alternating presentations. In a technique called *crosscutting*, the film editor can splice together two pieces of film that were originally shot separately to achieve this effect. The film version of *The French Lieutenant's Woman* (1981) is composed of scenes crosscut between the lives of actors who are making a movie and the movie they are making. As usual in such cases, the crosscut scenes invite the viewer to compare them: How are the actors like the characters they play? How is their romance offscreen like their romance in the movie they are making? The crosscut scenes visually comment upon each other. When you encounter crosscutting in a film, you need to analyze the effect to discover what kind of comment is being made by the director.

Cinematic Imagery

Film exploits all the sensory images that print does—only more so. In literature, for instance, you must imagine the sounds of raging battle, whereas the director of a war movie decides exactly the sounds you will hear: Will the roar of cannons fill your eardrums? Will the noise fade so that you can hear two soldiers speaking to each other in a foxhole?

Or will the battle rage silently on screen while you hear delicate chamber music in ironic juxtaposition? Through its greater power over your vision and hearing and as compensation for its weakness in portraying intellectual introspection, film usually has more pervasive and powerful imagery than literature does.

Imagery in the Film Taxi Driver

Let's examine the opening sequence of Martin Scorsese's *Taxi Driver* (1976) as an example of imagery in film. (A *sequence* is a series of related shots, somewhat like a scene in a play.) The image of the taxi moving down a dirty city street in the rainy night presents various kinds of sensory appeal. Visually, smoke, subway steam, and car exhaust puff across the screen, parting to reveal rain-slick surfaces that reflect garishly colored New York City lights. The camera first looks at the taxi from street level, a low angle that makes the car look overpowering and monstrous. (In general, a low camera angle makes objects or people seem to dominate; a high camera angle, as though from the ceiling or sky, seems to minimize the scene below, giving a feeling of detachment.)

Another great burst of steam obscures the scene, and then parts to show a close-up of the driver's lined, tense face lit with the city's red neon lights. Then we are inside the taxi looking out at the lights through the windshield, blurred by rain. Another cloud of exhaust, dyed red by the lights, fades to a blurry line of people crossing the street in eerie silence. We see the taxi driver's face again, his eyes tracking as he watches the people in the crosswalk. The red lights reflect in his glistening eyes.

The scene's auditory appeal is strong, beginning with snare drums and horns, threatening and slightly jazzy, like music in a smoke-filled bar late at night. When the picture changes to the driver's face, a more romantic, meditative saxophone theme comes in over the drums and horns. The music makes us uneasy because the two themes are vaguely at odds with each other. Street noise, which realistically would be loud, is mysteriously absent. The camera travels slowly along with the taxi, giving a kinetic sense of ponderous movement that seems ominous. The incessant rain gives a clammy, chill, tactile impression, especially since none of the people on the street seem dressed for it.

A Freudian approach would surely see the long, heavy taxi thrusting through the traffic as phallic. An archetypal approach would define the dark, seething scene with its ominous red glow as a classic vision of the inferno. The scene's images work together to impart an overall menacing impression. This sequence sets the mood and atmosphere of *Taxi Driver*, a work that presents a grim, hellish view of urban society. These images may even prove to be a foreshadowing of the dark and violent climax of the film.

Motif and Symbol

Imagery in film can be repeated or emphasized (just as in literature) to the point at which it becomes a motif or a symbol; that is, it carries more meaning than mere sensory impression. A certain low, pulsing musical motif in *Jaws* (1975) lifted people from their theater seats in fear as it warned film viewers (but not ill-fated swimmers) that the monster shark was nearby. And many people hum the opening bars of *The Twilight Zone*'s theme when something odd or eerie happens. Visual motifs, of course, figure strongly as well. The neon lights that we see in the opening of *Taxi Driver* recur throughout the film, gaining added meaning as symbols of the sleazy, cheap "scum of the streets" that the taxi driver despises. The color red also recurs, becoming strongly associated with sexuality.

Director's Techniques

It is often helpful to think of the elements you notice in a film as choices that the director made over other possible ways of putting the scene together—as, for example, the choice of a low camera angle to make the taxi loom ominously large in the scene discussed above. The selection of background music for each sequence is significant. Ask yourself, does the music work with or against the visual image? Directors often select details to produce visual irony; for instance, the kidnappers in *Ruthless People* (1986) wear children's Donald Duck masks. And remember that the conversations you hear in any film are carefully selected to stand out among the hundreds of sounds that would be heard in a real situation. Robert Altman proves this rule by exception in films like *Nashville* (1975) and *A Wedding* (1978), in which people talking at the same time blur and drown one another out, as they do in real life. Instead of letting you clearly hear a key conversation taking place at the party, Altman makes you struggle to piece it together over the surrounding hubbub. Thus, Altman portrays the social order as a confused babble, frustrating to those who try to make sense of it.

Visual Point of View

Points of view can be graphically suggested with admirable results in film. We, the viewers, can literally see the world from the point of view of one character when the camera acts as that character's eyes. In *Jaws* we sometimes see a shark attack from the shark's point of view, underwater. The classic mystery *Lady in the Lake* (1946) maintains a single point of view with the camera as the narrator's eye; thus, the narrator remains unseen by the viewer except when he sees his own reflection.

Film technology allows the director freedom from the objective or dramatic point of view of the stage play. We can see the world as the narrator sees it: slow motion photography, for example, can present that psychologically endless moment as Rocky throws his crucial punch in the boxing ring. In the film *An Occurrence at Owl Creek Bridge* (1964), the seconds between the time Peyton Farquhar is hanged and actually dies are extended to fifty minutes depicting the fantasy that flashes through his mind in that brief time.

As in literature, point of view in film can be

1. *Omniscient*—we see events through various characters as the director selects;
2. *Dramatic*—we see events objectively, as though we were watching a play;
3. *Limited*—we see events through one or more but not all of the characters' eyes;
4. *Unreliable*—we see events through a character who may be self-deluded or may see events falsely (for example, one of the mental patients in *One Flew Over the Cuckoo's Nest* [1975] sees the ward filling up with fog, and so do we).

Style in Film

Just as you can probably recognize the writing style of a familiar author or friend, you can also identify the styles of certain directors. In writing, style is described by such things as an author's characteristic sentence construction and length, word choice, figures of speech, and even point of view. We think of Henry James's writing as having long sentences with many clauses and phrases, a sophisticated vocabulary, elegant metaphors, and frequently a limited, introspective point of view. In the same way, the style of Alfred Hitchcock is recognizable by its complex and intelligent camera work and film editing. The tower scene in *Vertigo* (1958) combines an odd angle with a camera moving backward and a zoom lens moving forward at the same time to reproduce the queasy feeling of fear of heights. The grisly murder in the shower in *Psycho* (1960), less than a minute long, consists of over seventy separate shots spliced together for a vision of gruesomeness and panic that many viewers will remember every time they check into a motel. Hitchcock's style is also characterized by imbuing everyday objects like telephones and eyeglasses with significance, using color symbolically, and employing visual irony. As with literary style, a discussion of a film style must always relate to its content: Hitchcock's style reflects paranoia and anxiety to make his thrillers more thoroughly frightening.

Characterization in Film

Characters' motivations in film must be (or become) clear and adequate to explain their actions, just as in literature. In film, as in life, if a woman sacrifices her well-being for a good-for-nothing man, we are frustrated if we can never fathom her motivation. Even an ill-advised, overly hopeful, or neurotic motivation will satisfy us better than none at all. *Casablanca* (1943) would not be as moving as it is if we could not see the profound attractiveness of both Rick and Victor, whom Ilse must choose between.

Characters in film also serve in various roles: major, minor, and as foils. Major characters are usually dynamic—that is, they change over the course of the film—while minor characters may be dynamic or may remain static, serving only to move the plot along or to add comic relief. Foils serve the same purpose in film as in literature; these minor characters provide a contrast with some major figure in order to bring the main character into sharper relief.

But characterization in film has another dimension that it shares with drama—the acting. As you watch, you usually approve of acting that is unobtrusive; you do not want to be consciously aware that the actor is a person separate from the character. If you do have this awareness, as you may in movies like *Planet of the Dinosaurs* (1980), you may conclude that the acting is wooden, the characters misinterpreted, the film miscast, or the screenplay unactable. Even the plastic dinosaurs sometimes look embarrassed.

Setting in Film

Like sound, setting works with or against action in film. A beautiful outdoor setting can be perfect for a romantic love scene; on the other hand, a romantic love scene set in a crowded bomb shelter has a certain poignancy; and a romantic love scene set in a '74 Pinto in the Seven-Eleven parking lot provides some sort of comment on the situation—probably humorous. How much of the setting you see may be significant. Ingmar Bergman's *Scenes from a Marriage* (1973) is predominantly a "talking heads" movie, in which the characters' faces usually fill the screen. This film, as the title implies, suggests that the scenes it shows are universal; thus, the setting in time and place is unimportant. On the other hand, *The Bostonians* (1984), another film whose main business is talk, presents us with lush and detailed period interiors and trappings of everyday life in the late 1870s. In this film the historical and social setting is quite important to our understanding of the main female characters as early feminists. Also, Olive Chancellor's wealth must contrast with Basil Ransom's poverty in order for viewers to appreciate the hard choice that the lovely Verena Tarrant must make.

Theme in Film

The above examples show how technique relates to theme and form to content. As with a literary work, you need to think carefully about every element of a film in order to arrive at a statement of theme. Films, like novels, can have more than one theme. *Kiss of the Spider Woman* (1985) expresses a subtle feminist theme through its presentation of the kind, witty, and ultimately noble homosexual whose stated values are female. Incorporated into this same theme is a plea for tolerance toward gays. And yet the film also, and more obviously, provides a searing condemnation of fascist political oppression.

As you are searching for theme in a film, ask yourself the questions at the end of this chapter, and speculate on the significance of your responses. Try to discover how all the elements fit together into a meaningful whole. Analyzing film can be a lively, interesting enterprise, but in order to produce a good piece of writing about film, you should relate your discussion to the overall meaning of the work.

How to Study a Film

Until recently, film analysis was quite different from literary analysis in that we could not "reread" films like books; the number of viewing opportunities was also limited. This limitation is not so restrictive now. In order to write our analysis of the opening of *Taxi Driver*, we simply rented the video and played it several times on the VCR, taking notes. We reran certain important sequences and stopped the film occasionally to examine an interesting frame (a single exposure on the film).

If this way of "rereading" is not an option for you, do some preparation before you enter the theater to see a film you may want to analyze. Reading over our generic questions, which follow, will help you to become sensitive to film technique. After you see the film, you should immediately take notes on details that may otherwise fade from your memory. Discussing your observations with an intelligent, sensitive friend directly after the viewing will help you remember and develop your impressions.

LIST OF QUESTIONS FOR ANALYZING FILM

1. Does the film follow the traditional dramatic structure? If not, how does it deviate? Why?

2. How do the camera work and editing mark the structural transitions in the film? Are these transitions important?

3. Is there crosscutting in the film? What comments do the crosscut scenes make upon each other?

4. What senses are most strongly appealed to in the film? What images are repeated and/or emphasized to the point of becoming motifs or symbols? What meaning do they convey?

5. Do the images (of sound, sight, taste, touch, smell) work together harmoniously, or do they work against each other? If they clash, what is the significance of this discord?

6. Do you notice the use of camera angles other than eye-level shots? What is their effect?

7. Do the camera work and film editing provide the viewer with a point of view at any time? What—or whose—is it?

8. Can you make any statements about the style of the film? For example, is the style characterized by long shots, talking heads, contrapuntal sound track (in which the sound is at odds with the visual image)?

9. Did the characters' motivation satisfy you? Which characters are static and which dynamic? Are any used as foils? Is the acting adequate? Which characters, if any, do you identify with?

10. What is (or are) the main setting(s)? How important is setting to content? How much of the setting do you see?

11. How do the observations you have made so far relate to the total meaning of the work? Can you state a theme—or perhaps several themes?

PART TWO

Writing About Literature and Film

Writing is inseparable from understanding. You have to understand a film or literary work to write about it clearly and convincingly, and when you write about a work you have to examine your perceptions and judgments about it. In other words, writing is discovery—figuring out on paper what to say and how best to say it. It is the exploratory nature of writing that makes it invaluable for developing and testing your analysis of a film or literary text. In fact, the best way to study literature or film is to write about it.

Writing is not a single linear process. It is more like a series of steps by which a writer moves from discovery and planning, through drafting and shaping, into revising and polishing the final copy. The whole activity is recursive: it is not unusual for a writer to repeat a step several times or to go back to an earlier step before moving forward again. Moreover, writers seem to work through the process differently—some spend a lot of time planning and organizing, for instance, while others plunge right in and find their way as they write.

Because of these complexities and differences, writing instruction usually deals with general features that seem common to all writing situations. But our approach to the writing process focuses on four decisions that seem especially important for analyzing a literary work or film: What should you write about? How should you organize your thoughts? How should you support your judgments? What conventions and procedures should you follow? These questions can be translated into our four major steps for writing about literature and film: 1) finding a topic (discovery), 2) planning the paper (organizing), 3) developing the discussion (drafting), and 4) improving the presentation (revising/editing). Keep in mind that these steps interact with one another and that they include smaller steps, some of which you can combine or omit. You should try to determine how these strategies fit in with your own writing process and incorporate those which produce the most effective writing for your purposes.

Chapter 5

Finding a Topic

Of all the decisions that you make as a writer, one of the most difficult is choosing a topic. You want one that is manageable, significant, and interesting; but if it is too easily managed, it probably will not be interesting, and if it has too much significance, it may not be manageable. Balancing these requirements can be difficult, but fortunately there are guidelines and strategies to help you in this first step of the writing process.

Sometimes the problem of finding a good topic seems less complicated because the teacher has told you what to write about. But writing assignments vary in what they demand and what they assume. You will still need to define your purpose, consider your audience, and search your thoughts before you go very far. For instance, let us say that your teacher has directed you to discuss two characters in a play that you have read. This general assignment does not really identify a topic; it merely marks out an area in which you need to develop your specific ideas. Even if the teacher restricts the assignment by asking you to compare and contrast the way the two characters deceive themselves, you are still expected to produce specific material about self-deception and the various ways it can affect human behavior. In other words, no matter how particular an assignment is, you must still discover and select the subject matter for your paper.

Determine the Purpose

One way to close in on your topic is to establish the general purpose of your paper. Like many elements in the writing process, however, purpose plays an ambiguous role. Because writing is both a way to show what you know *and* a means to discover what you know, one of the purposes of writing is to find a purpose for your writing. The sensible method for handling this paradox is to formulate a *working purpose*— that is, make a tentative decision about what you want to accomplish in your paper. As you work through the writing process, this general sense of direction will help you to gather and sort ideas, but you can also modify and refine this purpose as you generate information and decide how you will use it.

An essay about literature and film is almost certain to be a *critical* essay, one that attempts to analyze, interpret, and evaluate the work under consideration. The word *critical* here does not mean "finding fault"; in the context of writing about literature and film, the use of the term goes back to the root meaning: to separate, discern, or choose. You will be acting as a critic, making judgments and offering explanations about the selections you have read or seen.

A critical paper involves one or more of these three general purposes: *interpretation*—saying what the work means; *analysis*—explaining how the work achieves its meaning; and *evaluation*—judging the significance or effectiveness of the work. These purposes are not mutually exclusive, of course. Interpretation of a poem, for example, usually depends on an analysis of technical features (images, tone, structure, etc.); and evaluation of a film typically includes both the analysis of techniques and the interpretation of meaning. But you will probably want to decide which of these purposes you are most concerned with. Teachers of college-level courses in literature and film usually prefer a combination of analysis and interpretation.

Analyze the Audience

Unless you are keeping a journal or diary for yourself, your writing always has an audience—the person or group of people who will read it. You need to keep this audience in mind as you decide what to say and choose the best way to say it.

No doubt you already have considerable audience awareness: you would not write a letter applying for a job in the same way you correspond with your dear Aunt Hazel. But writing a class assignment presents a special problem in audience. You know that you are writing for your instructor, but you are also writing for a more general audience at the same time—for that hypothetical reader or filmgoer who knows enough about the subject to follow your paper and be interested in your views. If this situation seems perplexing, that is because this second audience—variously called "the general reader," "the universal reader," or "the common reader"— is essentially a fiction, although a useful one. It is helpful to imagine a reader who is reasonably informed and generally attentive, one who will keep reading your paper so long as it is interesting and worthwhile. If you can imagine such a reader, your writing will benefit from the care and honesty with which you address that reader.

While this theory may clarify your approach to academic writing, it does not help much with finding a topic that will produce a successful paper. For this problem you need to focus on the one real reader you know you have—your teacher. Your teacher is your most artificial and most attentive reader. He or she has helped you study the material you are writing about and may have even given you guidelines or suggestions on how to write. Your teacher is also responsible for evaluating your work and will read your essay no matter how bad or good it is. Because of this investment, the teacher will be eager to praise your writing when it is effective and come down hard on it when it disappoints. Thus, you need to think carefully about your instructor as you sift through the possibilities for a paper topic.

The prominent linguist and educator Paul Roberts has offered some sound advice to student writers about keeping their teachers in mind when selecting a topic. In an essay entitled "How to Say Nothing in Five Hundred Words" (*Understanding English*, 1958), Roberts says that a "rather simple way of getting interest into your paper is to take the side of the argument that most of the citizens will want to avoid." He points out that because teachers are up to their ears in papers on predictable topics, the less conventional views are bound to be refreshing. Roberts also advises student writers to "take the side that looks to you hardest, least defensible. It will almost always turn out to be easier to write interestingly on that side." This advice does not mean that you should try to characterize Lady Macbeth as a loving wife who just wants the best for her husband; but as you come up with ideas for a topic, be alert for ones that encourage you to take some risks.

Generate Ideas

Having considered your audience and tentatively decided on your purpose, you are ready to search your mind, your memory, and your notes for ideas to build an essay on. Inexperienced writers tend to think that preparing for a writing assignment is primarily a thinking activity. All they have to do is think about what they want to say and then put those thoughts down on paper. But the truth is that you cannot think of everything you are going to say before you start to write and you cannot easily convert your thoughts into writing. These are complex operations that require time and work; they may best be accomplished by thinking in writing.

Invention

The process by which you discover your topic and its important details is called *invention*. The modern term for it is "prewriting." Prewriting includes a number of techniques or activities that allow you to "walk around" a topic, to look at it from different angles, to take it apart in various ways. These exploratory procedures are especially useful for preparing to write about film and literature because they help you to unlock your memory, to recall details and responses that you may have forgotten, and to associate them with other experiences. Four valuable invention strategies are *freewriting*, *brainstorming*, *clustering*, and *keeping a journal*. You will not need to use all four, but you may want to acquaint yourself with each procedure to find the one that is most productive for you.

Freewriting

Many people find that they can bring ideas to the surface through *freewriting*, a strategy designed to "free" ideas from your subconscious mind and get them onto paper. This kind of writing is "free" in another sense—you do not worry about correctness, word choice, or organization. Your main objective is to write for a sustained period of time (ten to fifteen minutes) without stopping.

Freewriting can be completely open, or it can be focused on an object or concept. If you write without a focus, you really are fishing for something to say. You can start, for instance, with just the title of a poem or story or film and begin to write in the hope that filling the page with words will coax something from your mind. This kind of exploration may result in finding an interesting idea or a provocative phrase that you can write about in another, more focused freewriting. Or you can focus your first freewriting by starting with a pertinent question about the literary work or film. Questions about the main character (What kind of person is Walter Mitty?), about the speaker (Who is talking to the dead runner in "To an Athlete Dying Young"?), about the setting (In what kind of town does "The Lottery" take place?), or about the theme (What is the meaning of *Virgin Spring?*) make good focuses for freewriting.

If you use freewriting, remember that you are writing for

your own benefit; you are attempting to discover what you have in mind about a particular film or literary work. Do not think about where you are going or what your sentences look like. You will have time to read and evaluate what you have written once you have finished probing the topic.

Brainstorming

Another way to get ideas down on paper quickly involves *brainstorming*. This technique can be done individually or in groups of not more than five or six. Because brainstorming seems to work much better as a group activity, you may want to arrange a session with some classmates to toss around ideas for writing. You can help each other discover topics and then decide what ideas to use as development. This approach was what brainstorming originally meant when industrialist Alex Osborn created the process in the 1930s as a method for generating solutions to business problems.

You can also brainstorm in writing. Start with a key word or phrase, and try to write down everything that the term provokes in your mind. In brainstorming you can just make a list of words, phrases, and other fragments of information. In effect, you are engaging in free association, letting your mind jump from point to point without censoring your thoughts. Nothing is trivial in brainstorming; do not make judgments while you are jotting down your associations.

When brainstorming about a literary or cinematic work, you may need to find a key image or term to start with. You might use an abstract phrase like "Othello's jealousy," "Antigone's determination," or "Lord Jim's redemption"; or you can focus on a concrete item like the black box in "The Lottery," the strand of gray hair on Miss Emily's pillow ("A Rose for Emily"), the compass in "A Valediction: Forbidding Mourning," the gothic mansion in *Psycho*. The idea is to start with something you feel might be significant or provocative and to go from there.

After you have finished your brainstorming, you take a

look at what you have generated. What items seem to go together? What further connections do you see between related items? What ideas and terms do you want to develop? What theme seems to dominate your list? What material is surprising? You may decide to use most of the items you produced, or you may find only a few fragments to keep. But one of these fragments may point the way to a paper topic.

Clustering

A variation of brainstorming that some find especially effective for generating details is *clustering*. This exploratory procedure was developed by Professor Gabriele Rico and presented in her book *Writing the Natural Way* (1983). In this method the writer places a "nucleus word" in the middle of a page and circles it. Then, by radiating lines from the nucleus, the writer spontaneously records images, feelings, and abstractions, placing each item in its own circle. Each of these "satellite" items, in turn, becomes a new nucleus to trigger more associations, which are also attached by radiating lines and circles. In short, the writer has produced a lot of clustered details that can be incorporated into an essay. (See Figure 5–1.)

Marking the Text

Whether you are brainstorming or clustering, you can enhance the effectiveness of your search for ideas by correlating it with your reading process. As you read, mark the text by underlining an important phrase or putting an X by a striking image. You can put a vertical line beside an interesting passage or write a comment or question in the margin. When it comes time to brainstorm or cluster key words and ideas, you can review your marks and use them to guide your invention strategy. This procedure of marking the text while you read is an effective prewriting activity in its own right and can help you in every stage of the writing process.

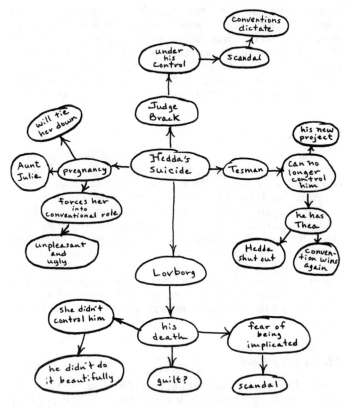

Figure 5-1 Example Cluster (on *Hedda Gabler*)

Keeping a Journal

Sometimes your notes to yourself may become too lengthy or too complicated to fit in the margins of the text. You should try keeping a journal as a means of recording what you were thinking as you read a selection or viewed a film.

Your journal becomes a source book of reactions, comments, and questions that you can use in future writing assignments. Most important, keeping a journal gives you practice in writing about the literary and cinematic material you are studying. In your journal you have a no-fault opportunity to try all sorts of writing, to become comfortable with terms and conventions, to express bewilderment and irritation, and to work out interpretations and judgments.

You are more likely to benefit from a journal if you write in it on a regular basis and use it in close connection with your reading or viewing. Record your thoughts as soon as you can, and get in the habit of drawing conclusions. A journal entry can also serve as an account of your reading of a poem or story. In such an account you can write down your initial responses to the work, tell how you analyzed individual lines and scenes, indicate what caused you trouble, and explain how you developed a tentative interpretation. You can also record what questions you still have and how you feel about the work after you have read it and thought about it. This procedure is helpful for reading a difficult selection; it encourages you to read closely and to interact with the text. In addition, you will become more aware of your own reading habits and strategies.

Chapter 6

Planning the Paper

Having examined your reactions, collected your ideas, and formulated a topic, you are ready to whip this material into shape. As you sort through the raw data and begin to assemble your information, you should expect to keep discovering new thoughts. And, if you see that you do not have enough ideas, you may want to return to the invention stage and generate more material. The possibility of discovery is present at any step of the writing process.

There comes a time, however, when you have to move beyond thinking of ideas and into planning how to present them. At this point some people prefer to launch straight into the writing, letting their thoughts arrange themselves as they go and ordering any disconnected ideas later. These writers seem to operate according to the principle expressed by novelist E. M. Forster, who asked, "How do I know what I think until I see what I say?" But this process can be wasteful; it usually means having to scrap large blocks of unusable material. Many people prefer to plan before they begin the first draft. There are several key decisions you can make to give yourself direction and save time. The first is to decide exactly what point you want to make in your essay.

Focus on a Clear Thesis

If you have not focused your topic by now, you need to do so. The key to a successful essay is a clear *thesis*, or controlling idea. You may have sufficiently limited the scope of your discussion as you were making decisions about purpose, audience, and approach; but before you get too far in your writing, you should try to state the main idea of your paper in a single sentence.

In order to be useful, your thesis should indicate the direction of your thinking—what you intend to say about the topic. It should be broad enough to include all the ideas that are necessary as evidence but narrow enough to focus your thoughts. If your thesis is too broad—like, for example, "Shakespeare's characterization of Macbeth is rich and provocative"—you may end up skimming the surface, never providing meaningful interpretation of the work. A more focused thesis for *Macbeth* might be stated in several ways:

> Shakespeare makes Macbeth's ambition seem human and demonic at the same time.
>
> Macbeth is more than just a victim of fate; the seeds of his evil are in his own personality.
>
> Shakespeare never really solves the problem of having a villain for a hero.

Notice that these thesis statements take a stand; they offer an interpretation that must be defended. If you are unsure about how to formulate a workable thesis, there are a couple of procedures that may help.

Posing a Problem

A good way to focus your topic is to pose a problem that you think needs to be answered about the work in question. A number of classic literary problems have kept critics and readers occupied with one proposed solution after another: Why does Hamlet delay in avenging his father's murder? Does Mrs. Macomber (in Hemingway's "The Short Happy

Life of Francis Macomber") shoot her husband on purpose? Is Satan the real "hero" of *Paradise Lost?* Who is the Dark Lady of Shakespeare's sonnets?

You don't have to try to solve a classic puzzle like one of these, but taking the problem-solving stance may yield a clear, useful thesis. You can ask yourself why a play or film ends the way it does or how a story or poem would be different if told from another person's point of view. One student, for example, produced a thesis for her paper about the grand-mother in Flannery O'Connor's "A Good Man Is Hard to Find" by asking herself why the Misfit shoots the grandmother at the end of the story. In another instance, a student writer focused an essay on "Sonny's Blues" by figuring out why the author, James Baldwin, chose to tell Sonny's story through the voice of the older, unnamed brother.

Relating a Part to the Whole

The best general advice we can offer to help you find a focus for your paper is this: devise a thesis that makes its point by relating some aspect of the work to its theme (i.e., to the meaning of the whole work). The following examples show how a broad topic can be narrowed by using the part-to-whole approach:

Topic: Shirley Jackson's use of symbols in "The Lottery"

Thesis: In "The Lottery" the author uses simple objects—a box, stones, some slips of paper—to symbolize the narrow-minded-ness and brutality that result from superstitious thinking.

Topic: The treatment of death in "Because I Could Not Stop for Death"

Thesis: By objectifying death in the figure of a genteel driver who takes a lady out for a ride in his carriage, Emily Dickinson stresses the inevitability, not the horror, of death.

Present an Analysis

The thesis statements that we have presented all take an analytical approach: they select one element of a work to look at in depth and then suggest how that part contributes to an understanding of the whole work. This approach— called *analysis*—is the most common way to write about literature and film, probably because it is both efficient and productive.

To analyze means to separate something into its component parts, but trying to write about all of the elements of a film or an extensive literary work would be impossible. So in an analysis you concentrate on just one of the components: symbolism in W. B. Yeats's poem "The Second Coming," for instance, or the use of the supernatural in D. H. Lawrence's story "The Rocking-Horse Winner" or the role of fantasy in the film *Kiss of the Spider Woman*. Then you can explain how this part contributes to the whole work. For example, you could show that Lawrence's use of the supernatural relates to the story's theme of greed and its effects on human beings by suggesting that greed is an insidious force that can destroy even the innocent. The aim of an analysis is to come to an understanding of a whole work by carefully examining some part of it.

Analyses can deal with any significant part of a work. These examples will show you the various ways you can approach literature or film through analysis:

1. *point of view*—the unreliable narrator in Ring Lardner's story "Haircut" enhances the reader's discovery of the main character's malice;
2. *symbols*—the repeatedly interrupted dinner parties in *The Discreet Charm of the Bourgeoisie* (1972) symbolize the useless, unsatisfying lifestyle that director Luis Buñuel is satirizing in this film;
3. *images*—the extraordinary images in John Donne's "Valediction: Forbidding Mourning" transform the poem's austere message into a beautiful expression of love;
4. *tone*—the mixed tone of "My Papa's Waltz" by Theodore Roethke makes two interpretations of the poem possible;
5. *character*—Nell, the "Woman of Brilliance and Audacity" in Stephen Crane's *Maggie*, helps to define the title character's vulnerability and to strengthen Crane's attack upon middle-class morality;

6. *cinematography*—the numerous long shot scenes in Mike Nichols's *The Graduate* show the main character against broad backgrounds and convey his rebellion against the larger world that is trying to force him into a conventional role;
7. *theme*—Eudora Welty's story "A Worn Path" demonstrates how love and perseverance can triumph over adversity;
8. *structure*—the short, choppy, seemingly unrelated scenes at the beginning of John Brunner's *Stand on Zanzibar* suggest the fragmented and confusing nature of the world of the future.

The possibilities for analysis are virtually endless, yet this approach allows you to limit your topic without sacrificing the opportunity to demonstrate your understanding of a work's general interest and significance.

Methods for Analysis

There are several ways to develop an analytical essay about literature or film. The three most useful methods are *comparison/contrast*, *argument*, and *explication*.

Comparison/Contrast

One way to develop your analysis is through comparison. Setting two works or two elements of technique side by side permits you to use one item to throw light on the other. Comparison involves looking at similarities; contrast directs attention to differences. But you can combine the two by showing how things which seem alike are really different, or vice versa.

The comparison/contrast method follows Plato's idea of finding out what something *is* by finding out what it is *not*. You can begin by establishing the basis for the comparison (the similarities) and then move on to the features that set the two works apart (the differences). For example, a comparison of Francis Coppola's *Peggy Sue Got Married* (1986) with Robert Zemeckis's *Back to the Future* (1985) would start by noting that the two films share the same premise—the lead character's going back in time to view his or her family origins. But the discussion would then focus on how each film exploits this premise in different ways for different purposes: the male hero in *Back to the Future* meets his teenage parents as strangers (before he was born) and changes their future and his own, but Peggy Sue becomes herself again in high school and discovers that she is powerless to affect the way things turn out. This comparative analysis might end with a discussion of which treatment of the time-travel theme is more effective and meaningful. Comparison/contrast is sometimes used to evaluate two or more works, although it is not always necessary to do so.

Organizing a Comparison/Contrast. There are two standard ways of arranging the material in a comparison/contrast. One way is to make all your points about one work first and then to do the same for the second work. This procedure is relatively easy to handle, but it does not allow you to emphasize the primary points of comparison. A second approach is to subdivide your main idea into major areas and consider each area as it relates to one work and then the other. This interlocking method allows you to keep comparing the two works all the way through your paper, but it can disintegrate into little more than a list of similarities and differences if you fail to relate the comments to a central idea. Here is a sample plan for an interlocking comparison of Richard Lovelace's "To Lucasta, On Going to the Wars" and Wilfred Owen's "Dulce et Decorum Est." The thesis is that the differences in time and audience account for the opposing views of war presented in the two poems.

1. Speaker's situation and audience
   a. Lovelace's 17th-century aristocrat hasn't been to war yet; he's addressing his mistress.
   b. Owen's persona has experienced the horrors of modern warfare; he's addressing those who glorify war.
2. Language and images
   a. Lovelace: eagerness, excitement, war as adventure; "new mistress" metaphor

    b. Owen: graphic descriptions of gore and destruction; drowning metaphor
3. Attitude toward dying in war
    a. Lovelace: it's honorable
    b. Owen: it's a big lie

Argument

If you want to persuade your reader to accept a particular interpretation or opinion about a work, you are presenting an *argument*, which requires that you give evidence and reasoning to support your position.

In an argument mere assertions are not sufficient. You have to gather your evidence and present it logically. A useful way to develop an argument was devised by philosopher Stephen Toulmin in his book *The Uses of Argument* (Cambridge: Cambridge University Press, 1958). His system is particularly valuable for examining your own arguments. Here is a simplified form of Toulmin's system, which asks you to answer the following questions:

1. What is your CLAIM?
2. What are your GROUNDS or EVIDENCE?
3. What WARRANTS (underlying assumptions) support the evidence?
4. What BACKUP exists to add further support?
5. What REFUTATIONS (objections) might arise in your reader's mind?
6. What QUALIFICATIONS do you need to make for your claim?

Let's say that you want to present an argument about Amanda in *The Glass Menagerie*. You can proceed by asking and answering Toulmin's questions:

1. *Claim* (the opinion you want your readers to accept)?— Amanda loves Laura and only wants what is best for her daughter.
2. *Grounds/evidence* (reasons for holding your opinion)?— Amanda says she always wishes for "success and happiness for my precious children" (Scene V); she enrolls Laura in business school, gets Tom to bring home a Gentleman Caller.

3. *Warrants* (assumptions that link your reasons to your opinion)?—Amanda means what she says; her motives are sincere; she honestly believes her actions will help Laura.
4. *Backup* (facts or details that demonstrate the warrants)?—Amanda resorts to selling magazine subscriptions to get money to help impress the Gentleman Caller.
5. *Refutations* (objections that you may want to anticipate in your argument)?—Amanda's motives are self-serving; she wants to relive her youth through Laura and to secure her own future by getting Laura employed or married.
6. *Qualifications* (conditions or exceptions that you might concede about your claim)?—Even though Amanda's motives are not entirely selfless, she does not give up on Laura, as Tom seems to; she does the best she can to break her daughter's dependency.

Explication

An *explication* is an "unfolding." In this method you proceed carefully through a text, usually interpreting it line by line. Because of its attention to detail, explication is best suited to writing about a short poem or a key section of a larger work. As an explicator you may look at tone, form, or setting; at the quality of the language (connotations, images, symbols); and at the way various elements relate to one another.

Although you may include paraphrase (i.e., "translation" of the original words into another, perhaps clearer language), your explication should be more concerned with what lies behind the author's choice of words. Through close, detailed reading, an explicator explores why a selection works the way it does, and thus helps to explain the meaning more powerfully.

Here is the way one student writer explicated the first few lines of Gwendolyn Brooks's poem "Sadie and Maud":

The opening lines state "Maud went to college./Sadie stayed at home." This initial contrast makes us think that Maud was ambitious and took action to get what she wanted, while Sadie was passive and had no real purpose in life.

Before going any further in his line-by-line commentary, the student stopped to make an observation about the poet's choice of names:

> If we think about their names, we might see an ironic twist to our initial impressions of the two sisters. "Sadie" has often been associated with a wild, loose woman, and "Maud" suggests a middle-aged lady sitting by the fire knitting a quilt.

The student continued by relating these observations to the next five lines:

> In lines three through eight we discover that our judgment of Sadie, based on the second line, was incorrect and that the connotations of the names are closer to the truth. Sadie was an independent, fun-loving woman who expected to get as much out of life as she could. The poet uses a metaphor of combing one's hair to describe how Sadie approached life: she "scraped" it "with a fine-tooth comb," worked through its tangles (problems), and "found every strand" (experienced all that she could).

The student explicated the rest of the poem in this way: He went to the dictionary to explain the unusual word *chit* (line 7); he noted that Maud isn't mentioned again until line 12 and is linked with her "Ma and Papa"; and he explained the meaning and tone of the "brown mouse" image applied to Maud in the last stanza. In his conclusion, the writer examined the interpretation that his explication had revealed:

> We can now see which kind of life the speaker is partial to. The center of the poem is devoted to Sadie—she was the one who had all the fun and got all the attention. Although some people might regard this as the wrong way to live, the tone of the poem gives the opposite impression. When Sadie died, she left as "heritage"—something worth inheriting—her fine-tooth comb. Her daughters "struck out from home" as if they could not wait to encounter the joys of being alive as their mother had been.

As you can see, an explication is easy to organize: you start with the first line and work straight through. But it also requires thought and a discerning eye. You have to make a lot of decisions about what to comment on and how far to pursue a point, and you also have to pull the various strands together in the end for some kind of general conclusion. This approach, if poorly handled, can be a mechanical task, but if well done, it can be an exciting and rewarding way to examine a rich and complex work.

The Film or Book Review

Writing a *review* of a work is different from writing a critical essay. In a critical essay you assume that your readers (your teacher, the class) are familiar with the film or literary work, and you offer your analysis or interpretation. In a review, you assume that your readers are unfamiliar with the work, and you offer a judgment in order to encourage or discourage them from seeing the film (or play) or reading the book. Although a review involves some interpretation and analysis, it does not usually explore the work in depth.

The main goal of a review is to present a judgment, but you must also provide enough information to allow your readers to decide whether they agree or disagree with your evaluation. The following excerpt from a review of *Platoon* illustrates how the reviewer praises the film and provides, at the same time, details and reasons to let the readers determine whether the praise is justified:

> *Platoon* captures the crazy, adrenaline-rush chaos of battle better than any movie before. [Director Oliver] Stone is ruthless in his deglamorization of war, but not at the expense of the men who fought there. His large cast is extraordinary: [Tom] Berenger and [William] Dafoe, both cast against type, are startlingly good . . . Charlie Sheen, a fine young actor, has in some ways the hardest part: playing the film's conscience. Stone has kept his alter ego deliberately generic—he's the educated Everyman—but Sheen brings him to life. His narration, in the form of letters to his grandmother, may seem overripe, even banal at times. Yet the movie needs this voice: the words are like a life raft that pulls us out of this fiery, hellish vision, and give us bearings. This violent, deeply moving elegy of war will leave you shaking.
> —David Ansen, *Newsweek*, 5 Jan. 1987: 57

Chapter 7

Developing
the Discussion

Now that you have some definite plans, you can move on to drafting your essay. As you proceed, you will need to answer some tough questions: How do I begin? What comes next? How much material is enough? Am I forgetting something important? How do I conclude? You should probably write at least two drafts, revising the essay until it expresses precisely what you want it to say as well as you can possibly say it. Remember, too, that writing stimulates thinking and helps to clarify it; so as you are drafting your essay, be prepared to modify your original plans if your writing leads you into a more effective thesis or structure.

Draft a Title and Opening

A good way to get started is to jot down a working title and sketch in your opening paragraph. Both of these items should be considered tentative. You need not come up with a stunning title or a perfect introduction; you can always improve them later.

A title should give some clear indication of your topic and, perhaps, your approach. For instance, "Laura's Self-Betrayal in 'Flowering Judas'" names the story and gives the focus of the thematic analysis. One student started with the title

"Phoenix's Journey" for a paper about Eudora Welty's story "A Worn Path," but halfway through her draft changed the title to "The Strong Character of Phoenix Jackson" in order to indicate more precisely what she was writing about.

The first draft of your opening works in much the same way: it points you in the direction you want to go. A good introduction should also arouse interest and set the tone for the essay, but you can make these improvements later. For now you just need a couple of sentences to set up your thesis. Here is the first draft of the opening for the essay on "A Worn Path":

> Phoenix Jackson has to overcome many obstacles during her journey to town, but she does not let anything stand between her and her goal of getting the medicine. This shows that she is a strong, uncompromising character.

This introduction is not elegant, but it serves the purpose of getting the draft under way.

Work Out a Structure

A traditional but effective structure for a critical essay includes three parts: the beginning (introduction), the middle (body), and the ending (conclusion). As we already indicated, the *beginning* of your paper serves to engage your readers' interest, to let them know what point you expect to make, and to give them any background they will need. The *middle* portion develops and supports your main point with details, examples, reasons, and explanations that make the general thesis more specific and understandable. The *ending* should relate your discussion to the theme of the work under consideration. In the next chapter we will offer specific suggestions for revising your introduction and your conclusion. Right now we want to give you some ideas for organizing the body—or middle portion—of your essay.

To help in drafting the middle of your essay, you may want to find some direction by jotting down a plan or outline. Such a device need not stand as an achievement in itself, with parallel headings and symmetrical divisions. It does not have to tell you exactly what to say at every point, and you can change it as you write if you think of a better way to organize your ideas. Your plan should, however, be clear and easy to follow. Here are two effective ways to guide your discussion without constructing an elaborate formal outline.

Plotting

Plotting consists of filling in blanks with topic sentences (main points to develop the thesis) and specific details (material to support the topic sentences). It looks like this:

Paragraph I—draft introduction, with thesis
Paragraph II
    Tentative topic sentence: _____

    Details to develop topic sentence: _____

To complete the schema, fill in the blanks with relevant ideas, examples, quotations. You do not even have to use sentences; you can jot down words and phrases that indicate what you plan to write in the draft. Follow this same procedure to plot all the supporting paragraphs you need.

Scratch Outline

A scratch outline is not as structured as plotting. It involves listing your main points, studying the list, grouping appropriate items, and determining an order for presentation. You can use letters and numbers to reorder the original list, or you can rewrite it. Here is an informal list that helped a student to organize the first draft of a paper on "Eveline," a story by James Joyce:

Eveline lacks the courage to leave with Frank.
1. Promise to mother haunts her
2. Can't leave father
3. Religious beliefs

4. How will Frank treat her?
5. Father getting old, less abusive
6. Comfortable at home

After studying her list, the student decided to eliminate item #6 (too vague) and to combine #2 and #5. She also looked at the order of her points and decided to arrange them more logically, a decision that we will now discuss.

Decide on an Order

As you draft the middle section of your essay, you will have to decide which point to take up first and which ones to use later in the development of your thesis. Ordinarily, you can arrange your ideas in two ways: logical order or chronological order.

Logical order involves presenting your points in a way that will appeal to your readers' intelligence and good sense. Many writers begin with an idea of moderate importance and work up to their most important one. The logic behind this structure is based upon the assumption that because your final point is the one your readers are most likely to remember, it should also be your strongest point. Here is how the student writing on "Eveline" rephrased the items in her scratch outline and rearranged them so that they moved from the general to the specific:

Eveline lacks courage to leave with Frank.
1. She is afraid to go against her religious beliefs;
2. She is afraid something will happen to her father if she leaves him;
3. She is afraid her mother's memory will continue to haunt her;
4. She is afraid Frank will treat her as her father treated her mother.

Chronological order, which is based on time, involves writing about events in the order they occur. Most narratives, such as short stories, novels, and films, use a chronological presentation of incidents. Your organization for a critical paper could simply follow the chronology of the work under consideration. Logical order is frequently preferable, though, since it provides a more analytical arrangement that will keep your paper from seeming like a mere plot summary.

Maintain a Critical Focus

Even though you arrange your ideas logically, the paper could still sound like a plot summary if you embed your critical insights in the middle of paragraphs. As you draft the body of your essay, you can achieve a critical focus by making sure that the topic sentences (usually the first one of each paragraph in academic writing) are critical observations supporting or relating to your thesis. (Placing the topic sentences at the beginnings of paragraphs helps your instructor to follow your thinking.) You can then use the details of plot, tone, style, point of view, characterization, or structure to support or prove the critical generalizations in the topic sentences.

Notice the difference between a critical comment and a plot detail:

> Plot detail: Jackson's story opens on a balmy summer day.
>
> Critical comment: By setting her story on a balmy summer day, Jackson creates a false sense of well-being.
>
> Plot detail: The oiler, who dies, was the strongest of the four men in the boat.
>
> Critical comment: The oiler's death is ironic because it upsets our expectations of survival of the fittest.

If you want to use both a critical observation and a plot detail in your topic sentence, be sure that the critical comment appears in the independent (main) clause and that the plot detail is placed in a subordinate position:

> Plot detail: The dog in "To Build a Fire" knows better than to go out in weather fifty below zero.
>
> Critical comment: The dog serves as a foil for the foolish man in Jack London's "To Build a Fire."
>
> Combined: In "To Build a Fire" the dog, who knows better than to go out in weather fifty below zero, serves as a foil for the foolish man.

Develop with Details

No matter what organization you choose for the body of your paper, remember to state each generalization clearly and to support each one with enough specific references to the film or literary work to be convincing. There is no magic formula for determining how much material is "enough," but you can try to stand in the reader's place and ask, "What do I need to know to understand this idea?" The typical college paper has three to five support paragraphs, and you will have to take into account your purpose, your audience, and your knowledge to figure out just how much development each point needs. The following sample paragraph is taken from the essay on "Eveline" and shows how the writer developed her topic sentences by using specific details, brief quotations, and her own interpretation:

> Eveline lacks courage to seek a life of her own because she fears that her father will not be able to cope if she leaves him. Her anxiety is heightened as she recalls that she and her brothers and sisters are grown up and that her mother is dead. If she leaves, her father will be all alone. She realizes that he is "usually fairly bad on a Saturday night" and probably recognizes that his drinking problem will not get any better if she leaves. Also she has noticed that "Her father was becoming old lately" and assumes that "he would miss her." As a dutiful daughter, Eveline seems to feel that going away with Frank means abandoning her aging father, and that may be why she has written a letter to him—to ease the blow of her departure and to soothe her own conscience.

Using Summary

In developing your ideas, you have to know when to summarize and how to use a brief summary to serve your analysis. You summarize an incident or scene to help establish a point or observation; then you can analyze or interpret that point. This pattern of summary followed by comment is used time and again, especially in reviewing literature and film. Notice how Pauline Kael, film critic for *The New Yorker*, uses summary to connect *The Godfather* with its sequel and to comment on the tone and impact of the second film, which she is reviewing:

> At the close of *The Godfather*, Michael Corleone has consolidated his power by a series of murders and has earned the crown his dead father, Don Vito, handed him. In the last shot, Michael—his eyes clouded—assures his wife, Kay, that he is not responsible for the murder of his sister's husband. The door closes Kay out while he receives the homage of subordinates, and if she doesn't know that he lied, it can only be because she doesn't want to. *The Godfather, Part II* begins where the first film ended: before the titles there is a view behind that door. The new king stands in the dark, his face lusterless and dispassionate as his hand is being kissed. The familiar *Godfather* waltz is heard in an ambiguous tone. Is it our imagination, or is Michael's face starting to rot? The dramatic charge of that moment is Shakespearean. The waltz is faintly, chillingly ominous.

Quoting from the Text

An important part of writing your first draft is finding appropriate quotations to support your ideas and judgments. Quotations provide valuable evidence—they let your reader know that your analysis is grounded in the text and is not based just on speculation. But you should be judicious in your use of quotations: use them only when they support an idea, and never include a quotation without commenting on it. In the following paragraph from an essay on *Antigone*, the writer uses several quotations to advance and support her analysis of the central conflict in the play, a conflict she contends is rooted in the gender of the participants:

> Antigone knows that she has violated the king's order not to bury her brother Polyneicês, but she seems not to notice that she has also violated the social code by stepping outside the boundaries of acceptable feminine behavior. Her act of defiance is courageous, self-reliant, and completely contrary to the obedience expected of women in her society. She fearlessly assures her sister,

Ismene, that "Creon is not strong enough to stand in my way" (Prologue, 1. 35). It is up to Ismene, then, to point out the obvious: "We are only women,/ We cannot fight with the men, Antigone!" (11. 46–47). A perfect foil for Antigone, Ismene epitomizes the good Theban woman—she is deferential, passive, and timid. Though she loves Antigone dearly, Ismene is still bound to her male masters and cannot follow her sister: "I must yield to authority," she says. "And I think it is a dangerous business to be always meddling" (11. 50–51).

Draft a Closing

After you have finished drafting your support paragraphs, you should put down a tentative conclusion. You do not want just to stop, as if you ran out of things to say. Neither do you want simply to reiterate what you said in your introduction. Instead, sum up, evaluate, drive home your main point. The student who wrote on "A Worn Path" concluded her draft in this way:

> With half her journey completed, Phoenix turns her thoughts to a Christmas gift for her grandson. Even though she has reached her goal and overcome many obstacles, Phoenix still does not think of herself. Her selfless dedication to her mission will give her the strength to carry on and complete her trip.

This was not the final version of the conclusion, but it gave the writer a feeling that she had completed her draft and was ready to review her entire paper.

A Final Word about Drafts

Writing a draft means different things to different people. Some writers expect their first draft to be rough; they do not expect it to yield much more than raw material and a general shape. These people often dash off their first drafts from start to finish in one sitting. Other writers combine drafting with revising and editing; they prefer to rework their sentences and paragraphs as they draft them. Recent studies of the writing process show that many experienced writers pause frequently when they compose—to rescan and perhaps reword what they have just written, to think about what to say next, to make changes before they move on. This drafting is what composition expert Mina Shaughnessy called "the messy process that leads to clarity" in writing.

You may want to assess your drafting procedures to see if pausing to rescan might help you to produce better drafts. Remember, though, that a draft is meant for you, the writer. Even if you polish as you go, your first draft will not be ready for your readers. You will need to review, revise, and retype or reprint your paper before you hand it in.

Chapter 8

Improving
the Presentation

You are probably relieved and pleased that you have completed the first draft of your essay. A large portion of your work is finished, but do not rush off to the typist or print your final copy yet. You need first to do a careful revision of your paper.

Re-See Your Writing

Revision involves more than just tidying your prose. You need *re-vision*—seeing again—to discover ways to make your writing better. Schedule your time so that you are able to lay the first draft aside for a while, at least overnight. While a draft is still warm from the writing, you cannot look at it objectively. Your fondness for a well-executed paragraph might prevent you from cutting it until you realize, in the cold light of morning, that it does not quite relate to your thesis.

As you examine your cooled-down essay, you may even see that while you were writing, your main point shifted somewhat. You may need to go back and alter the thesis or refine it; you may also decide to rewrite some material, cut some, or find new support from the literary work or the film. For example, one student revised her thesis about deception in *The Glass Menagerie* when she reread her draft and discovered that she had written far more about Laura, who seems the least self-deceived, than about the other characters. The student realized the irony in this discrepancy and decided to revise her essay in light of her new discovery. She did not have to junk everything in her draft, but she did readjust her support paragraphs to reflect her new insight about the ironic correlation between deception and self-deception that Laura seems to represent.

This student was able to get some distance from her writing, to look at it as another reader might. In revising, you should look at your paper from the reader's point of view. What questions might a reader want to ask you? These must be answered in the paper, because you will not be around to supply information. Will a reader find your essay consistent and convincing? Are there enough details, illustrations, facts, and evidence from the work you are writing about? If possible, get someone else to read your paper and tell you whether you have any lapses in logic or gaps in supporting evidence. You should plan to spend as much time in revising as you did in composing your first draft.

Outline the Draft

If you have written your paper without a plan, you should be sure to outline your rough draft. It may seem odd to make an outline *after* you have written a complete version, but listing your main ideas and supporting points will enable you to examine the skeleton of your draft and decide whether everything fits together properly. First, write down your thesis statement; then add the topic sentences of the support paragraphs and the main points that back up these topic sentences.

When you look at this outline, check first to see if every topic sentence expresses a critical observation relating to your thesis. If not, you should rewrite the sentence until it clearly supports your central idea—or else you should take it out. Then, examine your supporting details to see if any are irrelevant or overlapping and need to be cut. Next, consider whether your support is adequate. While it is possible to develop a topic sentence fully with only two subpoints, you will probably want at least three or four. Is there any important evidence you have overlooked? If you do not have adequate support for a topic sentence, perhaps you need to rethink it, omit it, or combine it with another idea. Continue through the draft, comparing it to the outline and looking for any digressions or unintended repetitions of material.

Sharpen the Introduction

As you revise your first draft, you will be trying to improve it in every way possible. You will probably need to look at your tentative introduction and see how you can improve it. Does your opening give your readers a clear idea of the topic and purpose? Will it arouse curiosity and interest, as well as lead into your subject? If you are not satisfied that your introduction accomplishes these aims, then you should re-write it.

One strategy for catching the attention of your readers is to use a pertinent quotation:

> "The less there is to justify a traditional custom," wrote Mark Twain, "the harder it is to get rid of it." This comment accurately describes the situation that Shirley Jackson presents in "The Lottery." Her story illustrates how ignorance and superstition become instilled in human society and lead to brutality and violence.

Another relevant quotation for an introduction to this same story might be Gathorne Cranbrook's observation that "The tradition of preserving traditions became a tradition." Useful quotations like these are available in your library in reference books such as *Bartlett's Familiar Quotations*.

You can also get attention by posing a startling question, like this:

> Why would the people in a quiet, peaceful village publicly murder one of their neighbors every summer? This is the shocking question that Shirley Jackson forces us to consider in her symbolic fable "The Lottery."

Or you can combine some suspense with a brief summary of the story's narrative:

> The weather is sunny and clear. The residents of a peaceful village have gathered for an important annual event. They smile and chat with one another, while the children scurry about in play. Then someone brings out a black box, and the ordinary people of this ordinary town begin the process of choosing which one of their neighbors they are going to stone to death this summer. This shocking turn of events is the basis for Shirley Jackson's story about the fear and violence that lie beneath the placid surface of human societies. The story is called "The Lottery."

Another way to introduce a critical essay is to use interesting details about the author or the story's background that relate to the focus of your essay:

> In June of 1948 *The New Yorker* magazine published "The Lottery," a story by Shirley Jackson. Within days the magazine received a flood of telephone calls and letters, more than for any other piece of fiction they had ever published. Almost all of those who wrote or called were outraged and bewildered. Why did this story prompt such reactions? Why does it still shock readers? The answers to these questions may lie in the work's strong symbolic representation of the pointless violence and casual inhumanity that touch all our lives.

Whatever strategy you use, keep the reader in mind. Think about reading an essay yourself: What do you expect from the introduction?

Indicate the Work and Its Author

One of the conventions of writing about literature and film is naming the work you are writing about somewhere in the opening paragraph. You are also expected to give the author's name in that first paragraph. You can see that all of the introductions above mention Shirley Jackson and "The Lottery." If you are writing about a film, you should give the director's name, and some film critics also include the screenwriter. After giving the full name in the introduction, you can then refer to the author or director by last name only throughout the rest of your essay. Do not use just a first name, unless the author or director is a personal chum; and do not use any titles like Mr., Mrs., or Ms.

Strengthen the Closing

Your conclusion is just as important as your introduction— perhaps even more important. You want to leave your audience feeling satisfied that you have written something worth reading, that their time has not been wasted. Do not give them a chance to ask, "Well, so what?" at the end.

You can impress your readers with the value of your discussion by reinforcing how your analysis illuminates the theme, or meaning, of the work you are writing about. This strategy may involve some restatement of the thesis that you advanced in your introduction. But try to avoid a simple and obvious repetition. Instead, combine your summary with a concrete image or detail that focuses your readers' attention on the point that you have made. One way to do this is to end with a key quotation from the work itself, as the writer did in this conclusion from an essay about James Joyce's "Eveline":

> Many who read this story will probably feel that Eveline should go off with Frank and leave behind her gloomy life. Careful readers, though, will see that Eveline cannot leave her family because she is female, because she needs the security of her home, and because she promised her dying mother to keep the family together. Eveline is indeed "trapped like a helpless animal."

Another way to focus on your main idea is to end with a thought-provoking question, suggestion, or statement. These last two sentences from a paper about Ring Lardner's story "Haircut" show how effective the rhetorical question can be:

> Does Lardner imply that human cruelty is inevitable? Is a neighborhood in a big city that different from the vicious small-town world of "Haircut"?

And here is the provocative last sentence of an essay about
"The Use of Force," a short story by William Carlos Williams:

> When Williams so vividly demonstrates how permission to
> employ force affects the doctor, the very model of humane con-
> cern, we shudder to consider what monstrous offenses the use
> of force may produce in less altruistic hands.

Whichever strategy you select, try to write a memorable
conclusion, one that reemphasizes your main point without
simply repeating it.

Integrate Quotations

Knowing that you have to use quotations for support, you
must resist the temptation to sprinkle them randomly
throughout your essay. As a rule, quoted items should be
brief and cited as support for your own words. Do not rely
on a quotation to make a point for you; state your idea first
and then bring in the quotation(s) to support what you have
said, like this:

> The most desperate character of all is the speaker of the poem,
> Lowell himself, who admits that his "mind's not right" (30). He
> prowls the local lover's lane hoping to catch some couple making
> love, but the locale is not particularly auspicious: it tops the
> "hill's skull" (26) at the place "where the graveyard shelves in
> the town" (29).

Make it a practice either to introduce all quotations or
to work them into your sentences. You are responsible for
making sure that quotations fit grammatically into your own
sentences. The following examples show you a number of
ways to integrate quoted material into your own prose:

> In real life Walter Mitty feels threatened by authority—or even
> competence—as we see in the episode with the "young, grinning
> garageman" who untangles the snow chains.

> Mitty's relationship with reality is so weak that at one point he
> finds his own wife "grossly unfamiliar, like a strange woman who
> had yelled at him in a crowd."

> We know poor Walter Mitty feels irritated by the competence of others: "They're so damned cocky, thought Walter Mitty, walking along Main Street; they think they know everything."

You may add your own words to explain a possibly confusing word by using brackets:

> In Mitty's view, the attendant "backed it [Mitty's car] up with insolent skill," although the insolence may be imagined.

Document Sources

Often you will need to cite the work you are discussing so that your readers will know exactly which passage you are referring to and where it is located. You may also want to use some ideas and opinions from other critics. If so, you are obliged to give credit to these writers and to indicate the source of this secondary material, in case any of your readers want to go to the original for further information. Most readers will not feel the need, but your citations will inspire confidence.

Your citation of sources should be placed in parentheses in the body of your paper. You need give only enough information to help your reader locate the source in the alphabetized list of "Works Cited," which you place on a separate page at the end of your paper. Usually, within your paper you can just give an author's last name and a page citation. The following examples illustrate the common forms of documentation for essays about literature and film. For more detailed information, consult the *MLA Handbook for Writers of Research Papers*. 2nd ed. New York: MLA, 1984.

References to Literary Works

For novels and short stories, give the author's last name and the page number (the author's name may be omitted if you mention it in your paper or if authorship is clear from context):

Rhoda Nunn emphasizes the importance of role models as she declares to Monica, "Your mistake was in looking only at weak women" (Gissing 316).

For poems, line numbers alone are usually sufficient to identify the source—provided that the author and title are given in your essay:

> Coleridge's assertion in "Kubla Khan" that poetic life is a "miracle of rare device/ A sunny pleasure dome with caves of ice" (35–36) proves paradoxical.

When citing a play, give the act and scene numbers (without abbreviations), plus the line numbers if the work is in verse:

> In *Othello*, Iago's striking comment, "What you know, you know./ From this time forth I will never speak a word" (5.2.299–300) serves as a philosophic closure.

References to Secondary Sources

If the author's name is mentioned in your paper, give only the page number in the parenthetical reference:

> D. G. Gillham remarks that the "male 'worm' " and "female 'rose' " in "The Sick Rose" have Freudian significance and "give rise in the speaker to half-hidden feelings of indecency, guilt, and fear so easily associated with sexual experience" (11).

References to journal articles are treated in the same way:

> Prospero's suite in "The Masque of the Red Death" has been described by Kermit Vanderbilt as "a metaphor of nature and mortality" (382).

In preparing your list of Works Cited, arrange all the works in alphabetical order by the authors' last names. Here are the entries for the sources cited above:

Works Cited

Coleridge, S.T.   "Kubla Khan."
    Poetical Works.   Ed. Ernest H.

Coleridge.   London: Oxford UP,
1973.   297-98.

Gillham, D.G.   William Blake.   Cambridge: Cambridge UP, 1973.

Gissing, George.   The Odd Women.
1893.   Rpt.   New York: Norton,
1977.

Shakespeare, William.   Othello.
Literature and the Writing Proc-
ess.   Eds. Elizabeth McMahan,
Susan Day, and Robert Funk.
New York: Macmillan, 1986.
679-761.

Vanderbilt, Kermit.   "Art and Nature
in 'The Masque of the Red
Death.'"   Nineteenth-Century
Fiction 22 (1968): 379-89.

Follow the Conventions

We have already alerted you to some of the standard components of a critical essay about literature or film: giving the
full name of both the work and its author in the first paragraph, quoting from the work, citing sources according to
accepted form. Here are some other conventions that you
should follow when writing a critical essay:

1) *Respect your readers.* You do not have to summarize
or quote extensively merely to familiarize your readers with
the work. Assume that they have read it or seen it at least
once. Your job is to enrich their experience by pointing out
insights that a closer examination has revealed.

2) *Use formal language.* Essays of this type usually employ
a style that takes a serious or neutral tone and avoids such

informal usages as contractions, slang, and sentence fragments (even intentional ones).

3) *Avoid second person*. Formal writing used to require a third-person approach:

> One can sympathize with Hamlet, at the same time regretting his indecision.
> The reader sympathizes with Hamlet's dilemma. . . .

But today most people accept the first-person plural in formal papers:

> We sympathize with Hamlet. . . .
> Hamlet gains our sympathy. . . .

You should, however, avoid the informal second person, "you." Even though we have written this text quite informally in order to speak straight to you, the reader, you must *not* write, "You can see that Hamlet is caught in a bind."

4) *Use literary present*. Events in a poem, story, novel, play, or film are described in the present tense:

> Marlowe's passionate shepherd *entreats* his beloved to "Come live with me and be my love."
> Raleigh's nymph slyly *rejects* these entreaties.

The reason for this present-tense treatment is that literary and cinematic action never ends—it occurs again whenever we read or see the work. The only times when literary present is not appropriate involve speculation about future events or consequences and description of something that occurred prior to the story's opening.

5) *Punctuate titles correctly*. Put quotation marks around the titles of short pieces that appear as part of a longer work, like poems and short stories: "The Passionate Shepherd to His Love," "A Worn Path." Underline the titles of longer works that are produced separately, like films, novels, plays, and long poems: *Casablanca, Adventures of Huckleberry Finn, Death of a Salesman, Paradise Lost.*

6) *Think of your own title*. Do not use the title of the film or literary work as the title for your paper. You did not write *Macbeth*; you wrote "The Reversal of Sex Roles in *Macbeth*."

7) *Choose precise terminology.* Do not call everything a "story." Although a poem, a play, a film, or a novel may contain a story, you should still call it a poem, a play, a film, or a novel. You may, of course, call a short story a "story." You will also benefit from learning to use the language of literary and cinematic analysis, as presented in Part I of this book. These terms will add precision to your writing and give you more control over the material you are dealing with.

Revising Checklist

1. Is the thesis idea intelligent? Is it clearly stated?

2. Is the main idea of every paragraph directly related to the thesis?

3. Is every paragraph fully developed with plenty of specific examples or illustrations?

4. Do all of my ideas flow coherently? Is every transition easy to follow?

5. Is every word, every sentence, completely clear?

6. Is every sentence well-structured and accurately worded?

7. Is my introduction pleasing? Does it make clear what the paper will be about without giving all the content away?

8. Is the concluding sentence emphatic or at least graceful?

9. Have I accomplished my purpose? Does the paper make the point I set out to prove?

10. Have I used formal English throughout?

11. Is my manuscript form acceptable?
    —Have I skipped three lines between the title and the first line of the essay?
    —Have I double-spaced throughout?
    —Did I leave at least one inch margins on all sides, including top and bottom?
    —Have I prepared a title sheet (if requested to do so)?

Proofread the Paper

When you get to the editing stage, you can cease being creative. Try to think not about the ideas you have written but about the way you have written them. In order to be a competent editor, you must train yourself to see your own mistakes. To avoid getting so interested in what you have written that you fail to see your errors, try reading your sentences from the last one on the page to the first, that is, from the bottom to the top. Also, if you know that you often have problems with certain elements of punctuation or diction, be on guard for these particular items as you examine each sentence. Here are some questions to ask yourself as you edit your essay:

Proofreading Checklist

1. Have I mixed up any easily confused words, like *its* and *it's* or *your* and *you're?*
2. Have I put an apostrophe appropriately in each possessive noun?
3. Have I checked to see that every sentence really is a sentence?
4. Have I carelessly repeated or left out any word?
5. Have I omitted the first or final letter from any word?
6. Have I used the proper punctuation at the end of every sentence?
7. Have I spelled every word correctly?

Sample Student Paper

The following essay was written by Elizabeth Curvey, a freshman at Eastern Illinois University. We have reprinted the poem she is analyzing at the end of her paper.

Admiration of a Woman

The speaker in Robert Frost's poem "The Silken Tent" compares a woman he admires to a soft, portable shelter. This extended metaphor conveys two distinct impressions: the femininity of a delicate, expensive fabric (silk), and the protective strength of a tent. The speaker admires his subject, the woman, for being feminine and strong at the same time; but it is her strength of character that inspires his praise.

Frost's speaker uses detailed descriptions of the tent to illustrate the personality traits that he most admires. The woman's poise and self-confidence are first conveyed in the description of the tent's movements: "it gently sways at ease" (4). And the depiction of the tent's "supporting central cedar pole" (5) seems to stress the woman's pride

and sense of self-worth. By comparing
the woman's soul to a "pinnacle"--a
sharp, straight, upright object--that
points "heavenward" (6-7), the speaker
reinforces his admiration of her inner
strength. But the hardness of this
image (especially when compared to the
soft silk and summer breeze of previous
lines) also reveals that the speaker may
feel intimidated in the presence of this
strong yet lovely woman.

The speaker's feeling of intimida-
tion may come from his realization that
everything the woman has and stands for
is the product of her own accomplishment.
This notion is expressed in the line
"Seems to owe naught to any single cord"
(8), a remark that implies that the
woman is self-sustaining and does not
rely on someone else for her esteem.
Yet the woman's self-confidence has not
made her insensitive to others. She is

connected "By countless silken ties of
love and thought/ To everything on earth
the compass round" (10-11). The speaker
seems to be saying that the woman is
capable of loving so generously because
she is completely self-assured. Her
ability to love "everything" also sets
her apart from any ordinary person; and
in these lines the speaker has set the
woman upon a pedestal, high above any
other woman he has known.

Perhaps the most significant compli-
ment comes in the last three lines of
the poem, where the speaker comments on
the woman's temperament:

> And only by one's going
>   slightly taut
> In the capriciousness of summer
>   air
> Is of the slightest bondage
>   made aware. (12-14)

Using the image of a summer breeze to suggest change, the speaker indicates that the woman handles her obligations with ease and equanimity. Once again, the comparisons in the poem present the subject as strong and confident.

Although the identity of the woman is never revealed, we can speculate that she is the speaker's mother: the poem expresses admiration, not the emotions of romantic love. But whoever the subject is, the speaker admires her strength of character and her quiet capability. Thus, the serious tone and dignified images of "The Silken Tent" transform a traditional love sonnet into a brief hymn of praise and quiet admiration.

[475 words]

The Silken Tent

She is as in a field a silken tent
At midday when a sunny summer breeze
Has dried the dew and all its ropes relent,
So that in guys it gently sways at ease,
And its supporting central cedar pole,   5
That is its pinnacle to heavenward
And signifies the sureness of the soul,
Seems to owe naught to any single cord,
But strictly held by none, is loosely bound
By countless silken ties of love and thought   10
To everything on earth the compass round,
And only by one's going slightly taut
In the capriciousness of summer air
Is of the slightest bondage made aware.

                              Robert Frost (1942)

Useful Reference Books

Cinema, A Critical Dictionary: The Major Film-makers. Ed. Richard Roud. 2 vols. New York: Viking, 1980.

Cirlot, J. E. *A Dictionary of Symbols,* 2nd ed. Trans. Jack Sage. New York: Philosophical Library, 1976.

Frazer, Sir James G. *The Golden Bough: A Study in Magic and Religion,* abridged ed. New York: Macmillan, 1922, 1958.

Frye, Northrop, Sheridan Baker, and George Perkins. *The Harper Handbook to Literature.* New York: Harper, 1985.

Geduld, Harry M., and Ronald Gottesman. *An Illustrated Glossary of Film Terms.* New York: Holt, 1973.

Gibaldi, Joseph, and Walter S. Achtert. *MLA Handbook for Writers of Research Papers,* 2nd ed. New York: Modern Language Association, 1984.

Guerin, Wilfred L., Earle G. Labor, Lee Morgan, and John R. Willingham. *A Handbook of Critical Approaches to Literature,* 2nd ed. New York: Harper, 1979.

Holman, C. Hugh, and William Harmon. *A Handbook to Literature.* 5th ed. New York: Macmillan, 1986.

Lazarus, Arnold, and H. Wendell Smith. *A Glossary of Literature and Composition.* Urbana: NCTE, 1983.

The Oxford Companion to Film. Ed. Liz-Anne Bawden. New York: Oxford UP, 1976.

Pickering, James H., and Jeffrey D. Hoeper. *Concise Companion to Literature.* New York: Macmillan, 1981.

The Reader's Encyclopedia of World Drama. Ed. John Gassner and Edward Quinn. New York: Crowell, 1969.

Glossary of Terms

Allegory A literary work in which characters, events, and often settings combine to convey another complete level of meaning.

Alliteration Repetition of the same consonant sounds, usually at the beginning of words:

> "Should the glee—glaze—
> In Death's—stiff—stare—"
> (Emily Dickinson)

Allusion An indirect reference to some character or event in literature, history, or mythology that enriches the meaning of the passage:

> In Eliot's poem, "The Love Song of J. Alfred Prufrock," the persona says, "No! I am not Prince Hamlet, nor was meant to be," suggesting that he lacks Hamlet's nobility.

Ambiguity Something that may be validly interpreted in more than one way; double meaning.

Analysis An approach to writing about a literary work or film that involves focusing on a significant part of the work and relating that part to the general significance and impact of the whole piece.

Antagonist The character (or a force such as war or poverty) in a drama, poem, or work of fiction whose actions oppose those of the protagonist (the main character).

Anticlimax A trivial event following immediately after significant events.

Apostrophe   A poetic figure of speech in which a personification is addressed:

> "You sea! I resign myself to you also—
> I guess what you mean."
> (Walt Whitman)

Archetype   A recurring character-type, plot, symbol, or
theme of universal significance: the blind prophet figure,
the journey to the underworld, the sea as source of life,
the initiation theme.

Argument   The main idea or thesis that a work presents; an
essay that supports an interpretation with evidence and
reasoning.

Assonance   The repetition of similar vowel sounds within
syllables:

> "On desperate seas long wont to roam"
> (Edgar Allan Poe)

Atmosphere   *See* Mood.

Audience   In composition, the readers for whom a piece of
writing is intended.

Ballad   A narrative poem in four-line stanzas, rhyming *xaxa*,
often sung or recited as a folk tale.

Blank Verse   Unrhymed iambic pentameter, the line that
most closely resembles speech in English:

> "When I see birches bend to left and right
> Across the lines of straighter darker trees,
> I like to think some boy's been swinging them."
> (Robert Frost)

Brainstorming   A form of invention that involves listing
words and phrases in rapid succession in order to explore
an idea or concept more fully.

Carpe Diem   Literally, seize the day, a phrase applicable to
many lyric poems advocating lustful living:

> "Gather ye rosebuds while ye may,
> Old time is still a-flying:
> And this same flower that smiles today
> Tomorrow will be dying."
> (Robert Herrick)

Catharsis In classical tragedy, the purging of pity and fear experienced by the audience at the end of the play; a "there but for the grace of the gods go I" sense of relief.

Central Point of View *See* Point of View.

Chorus In Greek drama, a group (often led by an individual) who comment on or interpret the action of the play.

Chronological Order The presentation of events according to the time they occur.

Claim The point or assertion that a writer advances for the reader's acceptance.

Climax The point toward which the action of a plot builds as the conflicts become increasingly more intense or complex; the turning point.

Clustering A variation of brainstorming in which a writer places a key word or phrase in a circle (as the nucleus) and adds related words and ideas in radiating lines and circles.

Coherence In good writing, the orderly, logical relationship among the many parts—the smooth moving forward of ideas through clearly related sentences. *Also see* Unity.

Comedy A play, light in tone, designed to amuse and entertain, that usually ends happily, often with a marriage.

Comedy of Manners A risqué play satirizing the conventions of courtship and marriage.

Complication The rising action of a plot during which the conflicts build toward the climax.

Conceit A highly imaginative, often startling, figure of speech drawing an analogy between two unlike things in an ingenious way:

> "In this sad state, God's tender bowels run
> Out streams of grace. . . ."
> (Edward Taylor)

Concrete That which can be touched, seen, or tasted; not abstract. Concrete illustrations make abstractions easier to understand.

Conflict The struggle between opposing characters or forces that causes tension or suspense in the plot.

Connotation   The associations that attach themselves to many words, deeply affecting their literal meanings (i.e., *haze, smog; female parent, mother*).

Consonance   Close repetition of the same consonant sounds preceded by different vowel sounds (*slip, slap, slop.*) At the end of lines of poetry, this pattern produces half-rhyme.

Controlling Idea   *See* Thesis.

Controlling Image   In a short story, novel, play, or poem, an image that recurs and carries such symbolic significance that it embodies the theme of the work, as the wallpaper does in Gilman's "The Yellow Wall-Paper," as the thunderstorm does in Chopin's "The Storm," as the General's pistols do in Ibsen's *Hedda Gabler*, as the grass does in Whitman's *Leaves of Grass*.

Convention   An accepted improbability in a literary work, such as the dramatic aside, in which an actor turns from the stage and addresses the audience.

Couplet   Two rhymed lines of poetry:

> "For thy sweet love remembered such wealth brings
> That then I scorn to change my state with kings."
>   (William Shakespeare)

Crisis   *See* Plot.

Critical Essay   Writing done by a critic, who analyzes, evaluates, and interprets a film or work of literature.

Crosscutting   A film editing technique. Pieces from two separately shot scenes are intermixed, creating a sequence that moves back and forth between them. The technique invites comparison and contrast between the two scenes that are crosscut.

Cut   In film, a simple method of moving from one scene to the next: one image ends and the next immediately begins.

Denotation   The literal meaning of a word.

Denouement   Literally, the "untying"; the resolution of the conflicts following the climax (or crisis) of a plot.

Diction   Choice of words in writing or speaking.

Dissolve In film, a transitional technique in which one scene fades from the screen as the next materializes.

Double Entendre A double meaning, one of which usually carries sexual suggestions, as in the country-western song about a truck driver who calls his wife long distance to say he is bringing his "big ol' engine" home to her.

Dramatic Monologue A poem consisting of a self-revealing speech delivered by one person to a silent listener; for instance, Robert Browning's "My Last Duchess."

Dramatic Irony *See* Irony.

Dramatic Point of View *See* Point of View.

Elegy A poem commemorating someone's death.

Empathy Literally, "feeling in"; the emotional identification that a reader or an audience feels with a character.

English Sonnet *See* Sonnet.

Epigram A short, witty saying that often conveys a bit of wisdom:

"Heaven for climate, hell for society."

(Mark Twain)

Epigraph A quotation at the beginning of a poem, novel, play, or essay that suggests the theme of the work.

Epilogue The concluding section of a literary work, usually a play, in which loose threads are tied together or a moral is drawn.

Epiphany A moment of insight for a character, in which the light of truth suddenly dawns.

Episode In a narrative, a unified sequence of events; in Greek drama, the action between choruses.

Establishing Shot In film, an overall scene or sequence that provides information about the location, atmosphere, period, or other background that the viewer needs for orientation.

Explication A line-by-line commentary and interpretation based on a close reading of a scene or a short literary work.

Exposition That part of a plot devoted to supplying background information, explaining events that happened before the current action.

Extended Metaphor *See* Metaphor.

Fable A story, usually using symbolic characters and settings, designed to teach a lesson.

Fade A transitional device in film. The image slowly disappears into a solid-colored or black screen in a fade-out. In a fade-in, the image slowly materalizes from a solid screen.

Falling Action In classical dramatic structure, the part of a play after the climax, in which the consequences of the conflict are revealed. *Also see* Denouement.

Figurative Language Words that carry suggestive or symbolic meaning beyond the literal level.

First Person Point of View *See* Point of View.

Flashback Part of a narrative that interrupts the chronological flow by relating events from the past.

Flat Character In contrast to a well-developed round character, a flat one is stereotyped or shallow, not seeming as complex as real people.

Foil A character, usually a minor one, who emphasizes the qualities of another one through implied comparison and contrast between the two.

Foreshadowing Early clues about what will happen later in a narrative or play.

Formal Writing The highest level of usage, in which no contractions, fragments, or slang are used.

Frame A single picture on the film. There are usually twenty-four frames in one second of film viewing time.

Free Verse Poetry that does not have regular rhythm, rhyme, or standard form.

Free Writing Writing without regard to coherence or correctness, intended to relax the writer and produce ideas for further writing.

Genre A classification of literature: drama, novel, novella, short story, poem.

Hero The character intended to engage most fully the audience's or reader's sympathies and admiration. *Also see* Protagonist.

Hubris Unmitigated pride, often the cause of the hero's downfall in Greek tragedy.

Hyperbole A purposeful exaggeration.

Image/Imagery Passages or words that appeal to the senses.

Informal Writing The familiar, everyday level of usage, which includes contractions and perhaps slang but precludes nonstandard grammar and punctuation.

Internal Rhyme The occurrence of similar sounds within the lines of a poem rather than just at the ends of lines.

Invention The process of generating subjects, topics, details, and plans for writing.

Irony Incongruity between expectation and actuality.

> *Verbal irony* involves a discrepancy between the words spoken and the intended meaning, as in sarcasm.

> *Dramatic irony* involves the difference between what a character believes true and what the better-informed reader or audience knows to be true.

> *Situational irony* involves the contrast between characters' hopes and fears and their eventual fate.

> *Visual irony* involves the incongruity between how something appears and how it really is.

Italian Sonnet *See* Sonnet.

Jargon The specialized words and expressions belonging to certain professions, sports, hobbies, or social groups. Sometimes any tangled and incomprehensible prose is called jargon.

Juxtaposition The simultaneous presentation of two conflicting images or ideas, designed to make a point of the contrast: for example, an elaborate and well-kept church surrounded by squalorous slums.

Limited Omniscient Point of View *See* Point of View.

Literary Present Use of present-tense verbs to write about events occurring in a poem, story, play, novel, or film.

Logical Order Arrangement of points and ideas according to some reasonable principle or scheme.

Long Shot In film, a picture seemingly taken from a distance: for example, people are seen head to toe, land-scapes from sky to ground as in a painting, rooms from ceiling to floor.

Lyric   A poem that primarily expresses emotion.

Metaphor   A figure of speech that makes an imaginative comparison between two literally unlike things:

> "New York is a sucked orange."
> (R.W. Emerson)

Metaphysical Poetry   A style of poetry (usually associated with seventeenth-century poet John Donne) that boasts intellectual, complex, and even strained images (called *conceits*), which frequently link the personal and familiar to the cosmic and mysterious. *Also see* Conceit.

Meter   *See* Rhythm.

Mood   The emotional content of a scene or setting, usually described in terms of feeling: somber, gloomy, joyful, expectant. *Also see* Tone.

Motif   A pattern of identical or similar images recurring throughout a passage or entire work.

Myth   A traditional story involving deities and heroes, usually expressing and inculcating the established values of a culture.

Narrative   A story line in prose or verse.

Narrator   The person who tells the story to the audience or reader. *Also see* Unreliable Narrator.

Objective Point of View   *See* Point of View.

Ode   A long, serious lyric focusing on a stated theme: "Ode to the West Wind," "Ode on Melancholy."

Omniscient Point of View   *See* Point of View.

Onomatopoeia   A word that sounds like what it names: whoosh, clang, babble.

Oxymoron   A single phrase that juxtaposes opposite terms:

> the lonely crowd, a roaring silence

Pan   A camera movement used in film. The camera swivels from left to right or right to left. The effect for the viewer is like turning one's head.

Parable   A story designed to demonstrate a principle or lesson using symbolic characters, details, and plot lines.

Paradox   An apparently contradictory statement that nonetheless makes sense:

> "Time held me green and dying"
> (Dylan Thomas, "Fern Hill")

Paraphrase   A restatement in different words, usually briefer than the original version.

Parody   An imitation of a piece of writing, copying some features such as diction, style, and form, but changing or exaggerating other features for humorous effect.

Peripheral Point of View   *See* Point of View.

Persona   The person created by the writer to be the speaker of the poem or story. The persona is not usually identical to the writer: for example, a personally optimistic writer could create a cynical persona to narrate a story.

Personification   Giving human qualities to nonhuman things:

> "Rain come down, give this dirty town a drink of water."
> (Dire Straits)

Plagiarism   Carelessly or deliberately presenting the words or ideas of another writer as your own.

Plot   A series of causally related events or episodes that occur in a narrative or play. *Also see* Climax, Complication, Conflict, Denouement, Falling Action, Resolution, and Rising Action.

Point of View   The angle or perspective from which a story is reported and interpreted. An *omniscient* or *shifting* point of view, which may include the author's comments on the action, presents the story through a combination of characters, shifting from one person's thoughts to another's. An *objective* or *dramatic* point of view presents the story directly, as a play does, using only external actions, speech, and gestures. A *central* point of view tells the story through the voice of a central character and is often presented as a first-person account. A *pe-*

ripheral point of view uses a minor character to tell the story. Both central and peripheral points of view are considered *limited omniscient* because they give only one character's perceptions. *Also see* Narrator *and* Tone.

Prewriting   The process that writers use to gather ideas, consider audience, determine purpose, develop a thesis and tentative structure (plan), and generally prepare for the actual writing stage.

Protagonist   The main character in drama or fiction, sometimes called the hero.

Pun   A verbal joke based on the similarity of sound between words that have different meanings:

"They went and *told* the sexton and the sexton *tolled* the bell."

(Thomas Hood)

Quatrain   A four-line stanza of poetry, with any number of rhyme schemes.

Resolution   The conclusion of the conflict in a fictional or dramatic plot. *Also see* Denouement *and* Falling Action.

Review   An essay or article that acquaints an audience with the general substance and quality of a work or performance.

Rhyme   Similar or identical sounds between words, usually the end sounds in lines of verse (brain/strain; liquor/quicker).

Rhythm   The recurrence of stressed and unstressed syllables in a regular pattern; also called *meter*.

Rising Action   The complication and development of the conflict leading to the climax in a plot.

Round Character   A literary character with sufficient complexity to be convincing, true to life.

Sarcasm   A form of *verbal irony* that presents caustic and bitter disapproval in the guise of praise. *Also see* Irony.

Satire   Literary expression that uses humor and wit to attack and expose human folly and weakness. *Also see* Parody.

Sentimentality   The attempt to produce an emotional response that exceeds the circumstances and to draw from the readers unthinking feeling instead of intellectual judgment.

Sequence A group of related shots in film, somewhat like a scene in a stage play.

Setting The time and place in which a story, play, or novel occurs. *Also see* Mood.

Shakespearean Sonnet *See* Sonnet.

Shot A continuous length of film shown without cuts. A *scene* is usually made up of several shots spliced together.

Simile A verbal comparison in which a similarity is expressed directly, using *like* or *as* ("houses leaning together like conspirators"—James Joyce). *Also see* Metaphor.

Situational Irony *See* Irony.

Soliloquy A speech in which a dramatic character reveals what is going through her mind by talking aloud to herself. *Also see* Dramatic Monologue.

Sonnet A poem of fourteen ten-syllable lines, arranged in a pattern of rhyme schemes. The *English* or *Shakespearean* sonnet uses seven rhymes that divide the poem into three quatrains and a couplet: abab, cdcd, efef, gg. The *Italian* sonnet usually divides into an octave (eight lines) and a sestet (six lines) by using only five rhymes: abba, abba, cdecde. (The rhyme scheme of the sestet varies widely from sonnet to sonnet.)

Speaker The voice or person presenting a poem.

Standard English The language that is written and spoken by most educated persons.

Stereotype An oversimplified, commonly held image or opinion about a person, a race, an issue.

Stilted Language Words and expressions that are too formal for the writing situation; unnatural, artificial language.

Structure The general plan, framework, or form of a piece of writing.

Style Individuality of expression, achieved in writing through the selection and arrangement of words and punctuation.

Subplot A minor complication which relates to the major plot but is not the main focus of the action.

Symbol   Something that suggests or stands for an idea, quality, or concept larger than itself; the lion is a symbol of courage; a voyage or journey can symbolize life; water suggests spirituality; dryness the lack thereof.

Synesthesia   Figurative language in which one sense impression is described in terms of another:

"hot pink" or "blue uncertain stumbling buzz"

Syntax   Sentence structure; the relationship between words and among word groups in sentences.

Talking Heads   A funny term for a film or sequence that consists of close-ups of people's faces as they talk, sometimes directly into the camera.

Theme   The central or dominating idea conveyed by a literary work.

Thesis   The main point or position that a writer develops and supports in a composition.

Tone   The attitude a writer conveys toward his or her subject and audience. In poetry this attitude is sometimes called *voice*.

Tracking   In film, a shooting technique in which the camera moves. It may roll on wheels or along tracks, or a person may hold the camera and walk or run. Notice the contrast between a track and a *pan*, in which the camera stays in the same place and swivels.

Tragedy   A serious drama that relates the events in the life of a protagonist, or *tragic hero*, whose error in judgment, dictated by a *tragic flaw*, results in the hero's downfall and culminates in catastrophe. In less classical terms, any serious drama, novel, or short story which ends with the death or defeat of the main character may be called tragic.

Type Character   A literary character who embodies a number of traits that are common to a particular group or class of people (a rebellious daughter, a stern father, a jealous lover).

Understatement   A form of ironic expression that intentionally minimizes the importance of an idea or fact.

Unity The fitting together or agreement of all elements in a piece of writing. *Also see* Coherence.

Unreliable Narrator A viewpoint character who presents a biased or erroneous report that may mislead or distort a reader's judgments about other characters and actions; sometimes the unreliable narrator may be self-deceived.

Usage The actual or express way in which a language is used.

Verbal Irony *See* Irony.

Verisimilitude The appearance of truth or actuality in a literary work.

Versification The mechanics of poetic composition, including such elements as rhyme, rhythm, meter, and stanza form.

Visual Irony *See* Irony.

Index